Warman's®
Shoes
FIELD GUIDE

P9-DGC-138

Caroline Ashleigh

Values and Identification

©2010 Krause Publications,
a division of F+W Media, Inc.

Published by

kp **krause publications**
A division of F+W Media, Inc.

700 East State Street • Iola, WI 54990-0001
715-445-2214 • 888-457-2873
www.krausebooks.com

To order books or other products call toll-free 1-800-258-0929
or visit us online at www.krausebooks.com or www.Shop.Collect.com

Cover photography by Holly Qualman

Library of Congress Control Number: 2009937515

ISBN-13: 978-1-4402-0898-0
ISBN-10: 1-4402-0898-0

Designed by Rachael Knier
Edited by Mark Moran

Printed in China

OTHER WARMAN'S TITLES

Warman's Barbie Doll Field Guide, 2nd Edition

Warman's Bean Plush Field Guide, 2nd Edition

Warman's Buttons Field Guide

Warman's Depression Glass Field Guide, 3rd Edition

Warman's Handbags Field Guide

Warman's Lionel Train Field Guide, 1945-1969, 2nd Edition

Warman's Lunch Boxes Field Guide

Warman's Matchbox Field Guide, 2nd Edition

Warman's PEZ Field Guide, 2nd Edition

Warman's U.S. Coins & Currency Field Guide, 3rd Edition

Warman's US Stamps Field Guide

Warman's World Coins Field Guide

This book is dedicated to my soul mates,
Doris and Drew.

Contents

"Foot" Notes 7

Introduction 9

It All Started With Barbie 9

Footwear Facts 10

Shoe Speak 11

A Journey of a Thousand Miles 13

Flats, Mules, Sandals and Slippers 14

Pumps, Platforms and Wedges 160

Boots 310

The Way We Wore 382

Famous Footwear 426

Resources 504

About the Author 508

Index 509

Andy Warhol (American 1928-1987), offset lithograph with hand coloring on paper, inscribed "Gee, Merrie Shoes" **$5,078**

Courtesy Heritage Auction Galleries

" See a shoe and pick it up and all day long you'll have good luck. "

— *Andy Warhol*

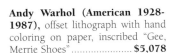

"Foot" Notes

Very special thanks to my fashion photographer and "sole sister," Holly Qualman, for her vision and tireless effort in making all of her shoe images walk the walk.

Most sincere gratitude to collector and shoe aficionado, Rebecca L'Ecuyer, for making her shoe-utopia available to me during my sole searching for some of the finest examples this book has to offer.

I am indebted to my many friends and colleagues at the following auction houses for the expert images that they provided: Sotheby's New York; Doyle New York; Julien's Auctions, Hollywood, Calif.; Heritage Auction Galleries, Dallas; Freeman's, Philadelphia; Leslie Hindman Auctioneers, Chicago.

Also, thanks to Dawn Nelson Steckmesser at Timeless Treasures Vintage Clothing Boutique, Manitowoc, Wis.; and Stacy LoAlbo, author of *Vintage Fashion Accessories* (2009 Krause Publications).

Lastly, I would like to extend warm appreciation to my friend, colleague and editor extraordinaire, Mark Moran, of Krause Publications. Knowing my passion for this subject, Mark invited me to collaborate on this pleasurable project. He dedicated many painstaking hours making sure we "put our best foot forward."

I guess I always had a little "girlie" side who liked Barbie. Barbie needs to wear great shoes because every girl needs to wear great shoes.

– Christian Louboutin

Barbie's pink sparkle pump.

Introduction

IT ALL STARTED WITH BARBIE ...

Like many young girls, my passion for shoes probably started when I began dressing my Barbie doll for a night out on the town with Ken.

I had miniature Barbie shoes in virtually every color of the rainbow, but my favorite ones were her florescent hot pink sparkle stiletto pumps. Right then and there, I knew that when I grew up, I wanted to wear great shoes like Barbie.

Today, owning a collection of great shoes in various styles and colors has gone from being considered a sign of excess to a rite of passage for the American woman. Take Carrie Bradshaw, for instance, of "Sex and the City," who mused about her wicked shoe craving: "The fact is, sometimes it's hard to walk in a single woman's shoes. That's why we need really special ones now and then — to make the walk a little more fun."

Whether you are looking for button boots from the Edwardian era or hot pink leather and rhinestone-studded platform mules with talon choc heels, *Warman's Shoes Field Guide* will help satisfy that inner shoe craving and make the walk a little more fun.

Hot pink Barbie shoe ornament, 2009 .... **$15**

FOOTWEAR FACTS ...

In most parts of the world (Asia, Eastern Europe, parts of the Middle East and Africa, much of northern Europe and Canada, as well as Alaska) it is customary to remove shoes when entering a house.

In some areas of the United States, especially the Midwest, it is expected that visitors remove their shoes unless a host specifically invites them to leave their shoes on. People do this to avoid bringing dirt, mud or snow into the house. For some societies, including those in Asia, indoor footwear may be provided for guests.

In the Middle East, parts of Africa, Korea and Thailand, it is considered rude to show the soles of the feet to others (even accidentally, such as by crossing the legs).

Shoe throwing is a great insult in some areas in the Middle East and in India. In addition, in Thailand, it is an extreme insult for the foot, socks or shoes to touch someone's head or be placed over it.

SHOE SPEAK

Beatle Boots * Bootie * Bootleg * Boudoir Slipper
Comma Heel * Cowboy Boots * Dance the Blues
Diamonds on the Soles of Her Shoes * Exotic Skins
Fantastic * Fetish * FLATS * Flip Flops
Footloose * FOOTNOTES * Foxy
Freakin'-Fabulous * GLADIATOR * Glamorous
Godfather of Sole * GO-GO BOOTS * Great Toe Cleavage
High-Heel Sneakers * Hurt to Wear but I Don't Care
Kick It * Kitten Heel * Mary Janes * Metallic
Mules * Never Touch Pavement * Peek Toe
Pilgrim Pumps * Platforms * Prozac for Feet * Sandals
Sexy * Shoeshine * Slingback * So Not Practical
Solemate * Sparkly * Spectators
Spring-O-Lators * STILETTO * Stocking Boots
Strappy * Style vs. Function * TWO MONTHS' RENT
Vintage * Walk a Mile in Her Shoes * WAY TOO HIGH
WEDGES * Wicked Shoe Craving

Red velvet "Spring-O-
Lator" sandal.
(see page 32)

A JOURNEY OF A THOUSAND MILES
BEGINS WITH A SINGLE STEP...

Warman's Shoes Field Guide is divided into four main sections:

The first and largest section focuses on shoes from roughly the mid-20th to 21st centuries, everything from fabulous flats, mules and sandals to sky-high stiletto boots, from drop-dead sexy to Mary-Jane sensible.

The second section looks at "The Way We Wore," antique footwear from around the world dating from the 18th, 19th and early 20th centuries.

Mostly for fun, we've included celebrity shoes, featuring footwear belonging to stars of the stage, screen and professional sports.

The last section includes vintage art, advertising and objects related to shoes.

Flats, Mules, Sandals and Slippers

"High heels" were once classified as starting at only 2". The shoes in this chapter range from "sensible" — little or no height at all — to sky-high sandals and over-the-top goddesswear. Prepare for a riveting experience in footwear fun.

Nine West, black velvet sandals with gold trim and rivets, circa 2005 .... $900

Courtesy Rebecca L'Ecuyer

Yves Saint Laurent, Black and yellow stiletto platform sandals, 6", circa 2008.. **$800** *each pair*

Courtesy Rebecca L'Ecuyer

If someone were to walk a mile in my shoes, they might be surprised to find out my 5" heels are always comfortable ... metaphorically speaking.

– Jessica Simpson

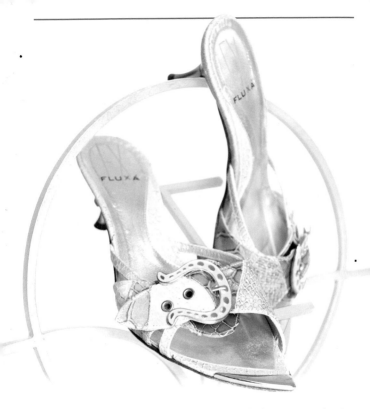

Fluxa, Italian multi-colored sandals with kitten heel, circa 2000 ..**$150**

Courtesy Rebecca L' Ecuyer

Via Spiga, Orange and white polka dot sandals, circa 2000..**$500**

Courtesy Rebecca L'Ecuyer

Prada, Purple velvet "tulip heel" sandals with ankle strap, circa 2008 .... **$900**

Courtesy Rebecca L'Ecuyer

Pierre Hardy, Wedge sandals with ankle strap and bubble cluster, "cosmic caviar," circa 2007..............................**$900**

Courtesy Rebecca L'Ecuyer

Lanvin, Black leather platform sandals, circa 2006 .... **$400**

Courtesy Rebecca L'Ecuyer

Miu Miu, White canvas and black leather stacked sandals, circa 1998 .... **$200**

Courtesy Rebecca L'Ecuyer

Miu Miu, Black suede sling back stiletto platform sandals, circa 2008 .... **$200**

Courtesy Rebecca L'Ecuyer

Louis Vuitton, Black patent leather and pearlized suede stiletto platform sandals, circa 2008 .... **$1,100**

Courtesy Rebecca L'Ecuyer

Guiseppe Zanotti, black and white patent leather stiletto platform sandals, circa 2009.. **$900**

Courtesy Rebecca L'Ecuyer

Valenciaga, black and white patent leather runway sandals with chunky silver-trimmed heel, circa 2005 ....**$800**

Courtesy Rebecca L'Ecuyer

Yves Saint Laurent, black and white patent leather stiletto sandals with side bow detail, circa 2004 .... **$600**

Courtesy Rebecca L'Ecuyer

Louis Vuitton, black suede with gold leather trim stiletto evening
sandals, circa 2007 .... **$800**

Courtesy Rebecca L'Ecuyer

•

> *If the shoe fits, it's too expensive.*
>
> – Adrienne Gusoff

Prada, black suede with gold leather trim evening sandals with matching ankle cuff, circa 2008 ....**$800**

Courtesy Rebecca L'Ecuyer

*"When the world went to my closet to look
for skeletons, they found shoes."*

– Imelda Marcos

Pucci, black patent leather platform sandal with chunky heel and
multicolored plastic disk detail on vamp, circa 2004 .... **$650**

Courtesy Rebecca L'Ecuyer

Left:

Berry Burke and Mickey Starr, black satin "Spring-O-Lator" sandal with black organza flower, New York, circa 1950.... **$70**

Top:

Red velvet "Spring-O-Lator" sandal with black leather detail, circa 1950 .... **$70**

Foreground:

Black satin "Spring-O-Lator" sandal with rhinestone detail, circa 1950 .... **$70**

Courtesy Rebecca L'Ecuyer

"You can do anything, but lay off o' my blue suede shoes."

– Carl Perkins

Jan Josef, blue suede cutout sandals, circa 2000................. **$150**

Courtesy Rebecca L'Ecuyer

Dior, crocodile lace-up platform sandals, circa 2007 .... **$850**

Courtesy Rebecca L'Ecuyer

Blue pearlized leather "Spring-O-Lator" sandals, circa 1950s.... **$70**

Courtesy Rebecca L'Ecuyer

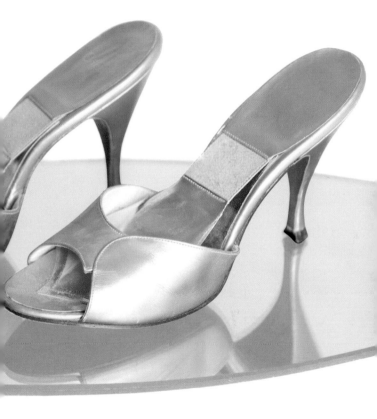

Kate Spade, sling back platform sandals with zebra bow detail, circa 2007 .... **$200**

Courtesy Rebecca L'Ecuyer

Black hounds tooth platform sandals, circa 2007................ **$90**

Courtesy Rebecca L'Ecuyer

Marc Jacobs, black and white T-strap sandals, circa 1996 .. **$100**

Courtesy Rebecca L'Ecuyer

Italian burgundy strappy sandals with gold and burgundy stiletto heel, circa 1970s.....................................**$200**

Courtesy Rebecca L'Ecuyer

Their costumes, as to architecture, were the latest fashion intensified; they were rainbow-hued; they were hung with jewels — chiefly diamonds. It would have been plain to any eye that it had cost something to upholster these women.

– Mark Twain, "The Gilded Age"

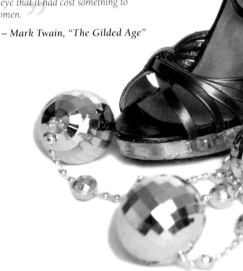

Di Orsini, white leather "sky-high" platform strap sandals, circa 1970s.. **$250**

Courtesy Rebecca L'Ecuyer

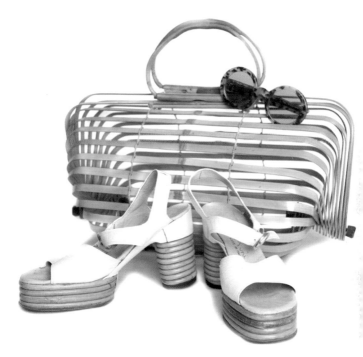

Garolini, white leather sandals with stacked bamboo heels, circa 1970s ....**$250** *shoes only*

Caroline Ashleigh Collection

Platinum mesh toe and ankle strap sandals with circular heel, circa 1980s **$750**

Courtesy Sandy Berman

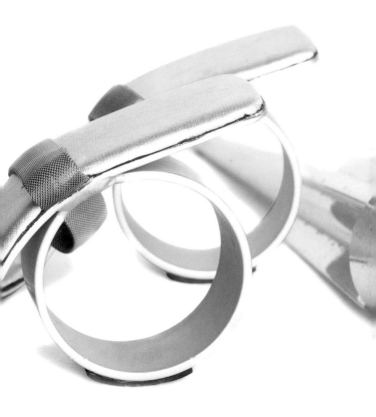

" The worst part about getting bags under your eyes is finding the shoes to match. "

– Adrienne Gusoff

Black suede "Spring-O-Lators" with gold trim and open-toe sandals with birdcage heels, circa 1950s **$550**

Caroline Ashleigh Collection

Black velvet platform sandals with ankle strap, circa 1940 ... **$400**

Courtesy Rebecca L'Ecuyer

"When in doubt, the best thing to do is just look in the mirror and say, "What shoes go with this Stress?"

– Caroline Ashleigh

Dolce and Gabbana, black leather ankle strap sandals with stiletto heels and gold spur and chain detail, circa late 1990s **$400**

Caroline Ashleigh Collection

"Exclusive," five jewel-decorated sandals made in the Philippines, circa 1970s .... **$50** *each pair*

Courtesy Rebecca L'Ecuyer

Young and Fair Casuals, Italian white patent-leather mules with applied flower, circa 1960s.. **$75**

Courtesy Rebecca L'Ecuyer

Hand embroidered black satin evening slippers with T-strap, button closure and silver Louis heel, early 20th century .. **$800**

Courtesy Rebecca L'Ecuyer

*Guilty! Can you imagine?
A man in a black robe and
brown loafers has the nerve
to tell me I'm indecent!*

— Nina Van Horn,
"Just Shoot Me!"

Gainsborough, gray suede and black leather ankle strap platform
sandals, circa 1940s...**$200**

Courtesy Rebecca L'Ecuyer

Five platform sandals, circa 1940's, from left to right:

Brown suede with applied decoration on heel, ankle strap and vamp, circa 1940s **$200**

Black suede ankle strap with applied beaded decoration, circa 1940s **$200**

Beige leather and suede platform sandal with ankle strap, circa 1940s **$100**

Red, green and gold snakeskin with ankle strap by Petite Custom Made Shoes, New York, circa 1940s.............. **$200**

Brown suede ankle strap with applied rhinestones and studs, circa 1940s.. **$200**

Courtesy Rebecca L'Ecuyer

Martinique, Black suede ankle strap platform sandals with heart shaped cutout design, circa 1940s.....................................**$200**

Courtesy Rebecca L'Ecuyer

Gainsborough, Pink suede ankle strap platform sandals, circa 1940s...**$200**

Courtesy Rebecca L'Ecuyer

Marc Jacobs, brown silk with gold leather detail and bronze-colored platform sandals, circa 2007 ....**$350**

Courtesy Rebecca L'Ecuyer

Chanel, black fabric evening sandals with pearlized white button detail, circa 2009..**$800**

Courtesy Rebecca L'Ecuyer

Floral platform sandals, maker unknown, 1960s .... **$85-$125**

Courtesy Timeless Treasures Vintage Clothing Boutique

Floral patterned silk and plastic sling-back sandals with applied
   bow, circa 1980s.. **$90**

Courtesy Rebecca L'Ecuyer

Alfred Ruby Inc. Detroit/New York, silk floral-design evening slippers with amber rhinestone buckle and black satin heel, circa 1940s...**$100**

Courtesy Rebecca L'Ecuyer

Woven raffia sandals with applied flower detail and cork heels.
Made in Italy, circa 1940s.. **$60**

Courtesy Rebecca L'Ecuyer

Saks Fifth Avenue, blue suede platform sandals with cut-away jointed wedge heel. Made in France, circa 1940s **$150**

Courtesy Rebecca L'Ecuyer

"When you have worn out your shoes, the strength of the shoe leather has passed into the fiber of your body. I measure your health by the number of shoes and hats and clothes you have worn out."

– Ralph Waldo Emerson

Saks Kay Shoe Salon, red suede wedge sandals, Detroit, circa 1940s...**$100**

Courtesy Rebecca L'Ecuyer

Black satin marabou boudoir slippers, circa 1950s **$45**

Courtesy Rebecca L'Ecuyer

Red suede platform sandals, open toe, Thom McAn,
circa 1970s...**$100-$150**

Courtesy Timeless Treasures Vintage Clothing Boutique

I'm having a wicked shoe craving.

– Buffy the Vampire Slayer

Zalo, teal leather strapped sandals with brown stacked heel. Made for Paradox, circa late 1970s – early 1980s **$100**

Courtesy Rebecca L'Ecuyer

Emilio Pucci, orange and yellow leather and plastic sandals with silver pedestal heel, circa 2004.. **$650**

Courtesy Rebecca L'Ecuyer

Charles Jourdan, white leather platform sandals with ankle strap and chunky heel, circa 1970s.. **$150**

Courtesy Rebecca L'Ecuyer

From Left to Right:

Oliver, black patent leather flats with white stitching, circa 2000 .... **$100**

Mosquitos, metallic gold and silver T-strap flats, circa 2000 ... **$60**

"Flats make you even more cat-like. Think of Brigitte Bardot in "And God Created Woman": when she dances in flat shoes, you have never seen anyone exude that kind of sex without having to do anything."

– Manolo Blahnik

Stuart Weitzman, orange patent leather flats with bow detail, circa 2000 .... **$200**

Stuart Weitzman, metallic gold flats with raffia and macramé bow, circa 2000 .... **$200**

Courtesy Rebecca L'Ecuyer

L'Autre Chose, Black suede platform wedge sandals with ankle strap and tan and gray bubble-cluster toe detail, circa 2005 .... **$300**

Courtesy Rebecca L'Ecuyer

Marc Jacobs, Black and white canvas platform ankle strap sandals with bow detail, circa 2005....................................**$250**

Courtesy Rebecca L'Ecuyer

Bebe, black leather and pony hair cuffed lace-up platform stiletto sandals with feather and bead detail, circa 2009 .... **$200**

Courtesy Rebecca L'Ecuyer

"I cut down trees, I wear high heels, suspenders and a bra. I wish I'd been a girlie just like my dear Papa!!"

– The Lumberjack Song (Monty Python's Flying Circus)

Gucci, black suede ankle strap platform sandals with stiletto heel and metal plate detail, circa 2009..**$800**

Courtesy Rebecca L'Ecuyer

Valentino, black suede and cutout white plastic platform sandals, circa 2008 .... **$600**

Courtesy Rebecca L'Ecuyer

Connie, amber plastic sling back platform sandals with cutout wedge heel, circa 1977 .... **$150**

Courtesy Rebecca L'Ecuyer

Manolo Blahnik, animal print pony hair sandals, circa 1990s ...**$500**

Courtesy Rebecca L'Ecuyer

" I know … the secret of toe cleavage, a very important part of the sexuality of the shoe. You must only show the first two cracks. "

Manolo Blahnik

Michael Kors, black patent-leather striped stiletto platform sandal, circa 2007 .... **$200**

Courtesy Rebecca L'Ecuyer

Terry de Havilland, gold snakeskin and silver leather ankle strap platform sandals, London, circa 2000 ....**$300**

Courtesy Rebecca L'Ecuyer

Gucci, bronze patent-leather and tortoiseshell platform stiletto sandals, circa 2009 ....**$1,100**

Courtesy Rebecca L'Ecuyer

Yves Saint Laurent, gold leather sling-back platform sandals
with raffia heel, circa 2006 ....**$500**

Courtesy Rebecca L'Ecuyer

Miu Miu, black, gold glitter and white patent-leather strappy stiletto sandals, circa 2005 .... **$700**

Courtesy Rebecca L'Ecuyer

"The American Shoe" with gold glitter, early 1960s.... **$35-$55**

Courtesy Timeless Treasures Vintage Clothing Boutique

"The easiest, sexiest, most perfect shoe is a flat sandal with a bit of sparkle. I love it."

– Giuseppe Zanotti

Miu Miu, Rhinestone- and glitter-encrusted sandals, circa 2005 .... **$500**

Courtesy Rebecca L'Ecuyer

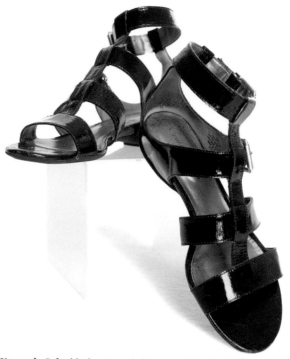

Kenneth Cole, black patent gladiator sandals, circa 2009... **$200**

Courtesy Rebecca L'Ecuyer

BCBG, tan and gold perforated woven leather sandals with stiletto hourglass heel and floral bow detail, circa 2004 .... **$250**

Courtesy Rebecca L'Ecuyer

Miu Miu, denim platform wedge sandals with leather bow detail, circa 2004 ....**$400**

Courtesy Rebecca L'Ecuyer

Kristoff, black suede and gold leather platform clogs with cork heel, circa 2006...**$150** *each pair*

Courtesy Rebecca L'Ecuyer

In a good shoe, I wear a size six, but a seven feels so good, I buy a size eight.

– Truvy, Steel Magnolias

Blue patent-leather flats marked "Holiday", late 1950s – early 1960s...**$30-$45**

Courtesy Timeless Treasures Vintage Clothing Boutique

I'd make a wonderful Lady Macbeth. I'll wear a pair of platform shoes or something.

– Bette Midler

Steve Madden, gold snakeskin stiletto platform sandals, circa 2000 ....**$200**

Courtesy Rebecca L'Ecuyer

Manolo Blahnik, tan and black leather lace-up spectator stiletto sandals, circa 1998...**$500**

Courtesy Rebecca L'Ecuyer

Enzo Angiolini, orange patent-leather platform sandals, circa 2004 ....**$150**

Courtesy Rebecca L'Ecuyer

White platform wedge sandals with floral bow detail, circa 2004 .... **$200**

Courtesy Rebecca L'Ecuyer

Hot pink leather and rhinestone-studded wood platform mules with bow detail and "talon choc" heel, circa 2004............ **$200**

Courtesy Rebecca L'Ecuyer

Cookies, hot pink plastic and acrylic platform mules, circa 2004 ....**$200**

Courtesy Rebecca L'Ecuyer

Charles David, black leather ankle strap platform wedge sandals with floral bow detail **$125**

Courtesy Rebecca L'Ecuyer

Charles David, black leather wedge sandals, circa 1999 .... $125

Courtesy Rebecca L'Ecuyer

Sesto Meucci, animal print patent leather mules, circa 1999 .... **$150**

Courtesy Rebecca L'Ecuyer

"The only thing that separates us from the animals is our ability to accessorize."

– Clairee Belcher, "Steel Magnolias"

The reason the Romans built their great paved highways was that they had such inconvenient footwear.

– Charles de Montesquieu

Paputsi of Greece, black leather woven cage lace-up brogues, circa 1940s..**$200**

Courtesy Rebecca L'Ecuyer

Chinese Laundry, orange raw silk platform sandals, circa 1999 ....**$100**

Courtesy Rebecca L'Ecuyer

Moda Spana, black and white leather checkerboard mules, circa 1995 .... **$100**

Courtesy Rebecca L'Ecuyer

Claudia Cuiti, black and white patent leather platform sandals, circa 2004 ....**$100**

Courtesy Rebecca L'Ecuyer

" If God had wanted us to wear flat shoes, He wouldn't have invented Manolo Blahnik. "

– Alexandra Shulman

Manolo Blahnik, black satin stilettos with rhinestone-studded buckle, circa 2005 .... **$250**

Caroline Ashleigh Collection

Christian Louboutin, champagne satin and lace strappy stiletto, circa 2007 .... **$650**

Caroline Ashleigh Collection

Fendi, leopard print, pony hair and patent leather platform stiletto sandals, circa 2009 .... **$800**

Courtesy Rebecca L'Ecuyer

Chanel, satin brocade and patent leather platform sandal, circa 2009 .... **$1,100**

Courtesy Rebecca L'Ecuyer

Charles Jourdan, silver and patent leather wedge sandals, circa late 1980s...**$350**

Courtesy Rebecca L'Ecuyer

Fendi, black suede and textured bronze leather platform stiletto sandals, circa 2009 ....**$800**

Courtesy Rebecca L'Louyer

Prada, yellow, orange and peach patent-leather T-strap, open-toe sandals, circa 2006 .... **$400**

Courtesy Rebecca L'Ecuyer

Via Spiga, black patent-leather stiletto sandals with black netting and acrylic flower detail, circa 2003.................................**$100**

Courtesy Rebecca L'Ecuyer

BCBG, turquoise wedge platform sandals with burgundy ribbon detail and stacked-wood heel, circa 2004..........................**$250**

Courtesy Rebecca L'Ecuyer

Nine West, tan canvas and cork ankle-tie platform sandals with open toe, circa 1994...**$100**

Courtesy Rebecca L'Ecuyer

Sensual Steps, plastic and acrylic platform mules with cabochon detail, circa 1990s **$100**

Courtesy Rebecca L'Ecuyer

Black and white striped mules with pom-pom flower detail, circa 2000 .... **$150**

Courtesy Rebecca L'Ecuyer

Nine West, silver leather platform sandals, circa 2006........ **$100**

Courtesy Rebecca L'Ecuyer

Marc Jacobs, red suede ankle strap platform wedge sandals, circa 2003 .... **$300**

Courtesy Rebecca L'Ecuyer

BCBG, black patent leather sandals with gold bubble cluster detail, circa 2007 .... **$200**

Courtesy Rebecca L'Ecuyer

*"What becomes of
the broken-hearted?
They buy shoes."*

– Mimi Pond

Black sandals with applied white floral detail, circa 2005....**$200**

Courtesy Rebecca L'Ecuyer

Escapezios, mint green suede booties, early 1960s....... **$35-$65**

Courtesy Timeless Treasures Vintage Clothing Boutique

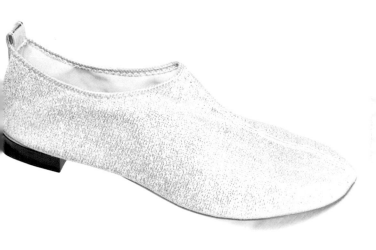

Silver metallic thread "space-age" booties, circa 1960s **$150**

Courtesy Rebecca L'Ecuyer

Chinese Laundry, red fabric stiletto sandals with red and white grosgrain ribbon, circa 1995 .... **$75**

Courtesy Rebecca L'Ecuyer

LaRose newspaper ad with matching red and white polka dot sling-back stiletto sandals with red bow detail........... **$700** *shoes only*

Courtesy Sotheby's

Bebe, floral print ankle strap platform sandals, circa 1990s ... **$100**

Courtesy Rebecca L'Ecuyer

Via Spiga, white patent leather platform sandals, circa 1995   **$100**

Courtesy Rebecca L'Ecuyer

Nine West, Raffia platform sandals with multi-colored raffia floral detail, circa 1995... **$90**

Courtesy Rebecca L'Ecuyer

DeLiso Debs, silk block print with slingback, late 1960s **$68**

Courtesy Stacy LoAlbo

Strappy peach rayon, chunky heels, mid-1970s.................... **$50**

Courtesy Stacy LoAlbo

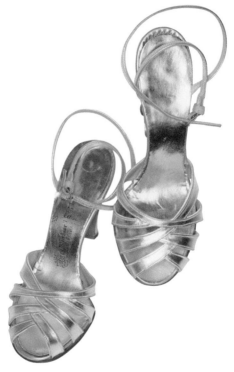

Silver leather ankle strap high heels, circa 1950s **$75**

Courtesy Stacy LoAlbo

Gold leather ankle strap high heels, circa 1950s................ **$75**

Courtesy Stacy LoAlbo

Palter DeLiso, hot pink metallic Cinderella slippers with detachable bows on the Lucite vamp, circa 1970 .... **$160**

From the collection of Incogneeto
Courtesy Stacy LoAlbo

Lucite vamp with rows of rhinestones, circa 1960s **$125**

Courtesy Stacy LoAlbo

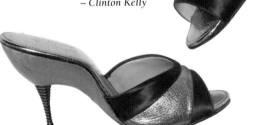

"*Sometimes comfort doesn't matter. When a shoe is freakin' fabulous, it may be worth a subsequent day of misery. Soak in Epsom salts and take comfort in the fact that you're better than everyone else.*"

– Clinton Kelly

Ferncraft Exclusives, rare "Marilyn" screw-like spike high heels, late 1950s...**$375**

From the collection of Joe Sundlies Vintedge
Courtesy Stacy LoAlbo

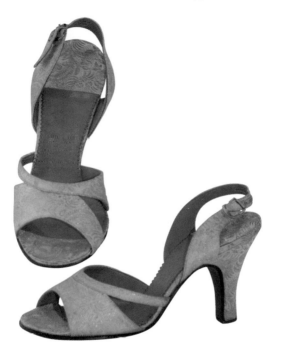

Gold and silver metallic brocade open-toed slingbacks, circa 1950 .... **$185**

From the collection of Vintage with a Twist
Courtesy Stacy LoAlbo

"I. Miller Beautiful Shoes" with pearls and steel-cut beading across the vamp, circa 1950s..**$165**

Courtesy Stacy LoAlbo

Lucite sling backs have pink leather heels and decoration, circa 1950s.. **$125**

Courtesy Stacy LoAlbo

Clear Lucite vamp shoes, with rhinestone design in a T-strap
formation, circa 1960s...**$175**

From the collection of Vintage with a Twist
Courtesy Stacy LoAlbo

Two-tone purple and lavender leather ankle strap heels, circa 1950s...**$85**

Courtesy Stacy LoAlbo

Red leather Mary Jane flats, late 1950s.............................. **$68**

Courtesy Stacy LoAlbo

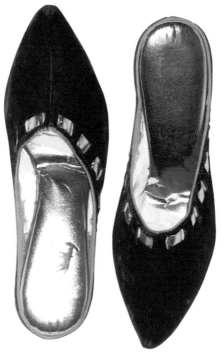

Hot pink velvet mules with a little "kitten" heel, early 1960s   **$55**

Courtesy Stacy LoAlbo

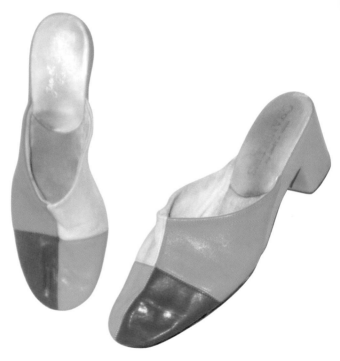

Multi-colored leather mules, 1970s.....................................**$55**

Courtesy Stacy LoAlbo

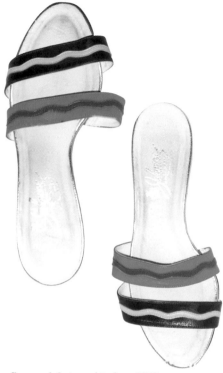

Leather flat sandals in multicolors, 1970s **$40**

Courtesy Stacy LoAlbo

Two-tone leather resort shoes with an open toe and layered wedge heel, 1940s..**$275**

From the collection of Incogneeto
Courtesy Stacy LoAlbo

French handmade pink velvet mules with black braid trim and Louis heel, circa 1935 .. .. **$245**

From the collection of Vintage with a Twist
Courtesy Stacy LoAlbo

Suede mules with embellishments and studded toe fringe, 1960s **$155**

Courtesy Stacy LoAlbo

Wedgic slippers in metallic brocade with peep-toe front, 1950s...**$80**

Courtesy Stacy LoAlbo

Woven black and white leather sandals, 1940s.................. **$89**

From the collection of Sue Stani at Somerville Center Antiques
Courtesy Stacy LoAlbo

Leather flats, colorful floral design and original polka dot laces, 1980s..**$68**

Courtesy Stacy LoAlbo

Pumps, Platforms and Wedges

Don't be afraid of heights — this section is full of uplifting experiences. But that's nothing new: As early as 1533, Queen Catherine de' Medici, the diminutive Italian wife of Henry II, King of France, commissioned a cobbler to fashion her a pair of heels, both for fashion and to suggest greater height and power.

Beverly Feldman, "I Love Diamonds" black canvas open toed wedge sandals with silver rhinestones, circa 2006............ **$150**

Courtesy Rebecca L'Ecuyer

Dolce & Gabana, black suede pumps with silver studs and bow, circa 2003 .... **$300**

Courtesy Rebecca L'Ecuyer

Steve Madden, black suede stiletto pumps with rhinestones and silver studs, circa 2003 .... **$300**

Courtesy Rebecca L'Ecuyer

Enzio Angelini, cheetah print ankle strap platform sandals with marabou pom-pom detail, circa 1995 ....**$150**

Courtesy Rebecca L'Ecuyer

Stuart Weitzman, leopard, zebra and giraffe print ankle strap sandals, circa 1995 ....**$250**

Courtesy Rebecca L'Ecuyer

Nine West, leopard print open-toe pumps..........................**$150**

Courtesy Rebecca L'Ecuyer

Stuart Weitzman, black and tan pony hair pumps, circa 2004 .... **$200**

Courtesy Rebecca L'Ecuyer

Michael Kors, black leather stiletto pumps with silver buckle strap detail, circa 2004 .... **$200**

Courtesy Rebecca L'Ecuyer

Marc Jacobs, black leather Mary Janes, circa late 1990s ...**$200**

Courtesy Rebecca L'Ecuyer

Embroidered shoes, 1940s **$100**

Courtesy www.freemansauctions.com, Philadelphia

Embroidered shoes, 1940s **$100**

Courtesy www.freemansauctions.com, Philadelphia

"French Room" Chandler's pumps with matching purse, barkcloth/leather, 1950s ....**$125-$175** *set*

Courtesy Timeless Treasures Vintage Clothing Boutique

Palizzio, mod pumps and matching purse, 1960s... **$100-$150 set**

Courtesy Timeless Treasures Vintage Clothing Boutique

Herbert Burr, black velvet and red leather pumps, circa 1950 ....**$90**

Courtesy Rebecca L'Ecuyer

Evins, mesh and rhinestone pumps, circa 1950s........ .... **$90**

Courtesy Rebecca L'Ecuyer

Ferantino, pewter leather pumps with matching handbag, 1950s .... **$100-$150** *set*

Courtesy Timeless Treasures Vintage Clothing Boutique

I think the key is, you have to have platforms, and then you can actually stand in them longer. If you don't have a platform, it's kind of hard to survive in a 6-inch heel.

– Rachel Zoe

Harlequin pattern suede platform teal pumps, circa 2009 .. **$400**

Courtesy Rebecca L'Ecuyer

Stuart Weitzman, retro '40s black suede platform pumps with red patent-leather detail, circa 2008 .... **$300**

Courtesy Rebecca L'Ecuyer

Andrea Pfister, Italian red, blue, yellow and green pumps, circa 1980s...**$90**

Courtesy Rebecca L'Ecuyer

Marc Jacobs, black and white patent-leather pumps, circa 2003 ....**$150**

Courtesy Rebecca L'Ecuyer

Gucci, black leather lace-up platform spectators with gold trim, circa 2007 .... **$800**

Courtesy Rebecca L'Ecuyer

Chanel, dove grey and black leather lace-up spectators, circa 2004 .... **$600**

Courtesy Rebecca L'Ecuyer

Renee Caovilla, black and white pumps with graphic design, circa 2005 .... **$400**

Courtesy Rebecca L'Ecuyer

Terrorism, hurricanes, and acts of God can't part a true Imelda from her shoes

— Author Jane Eldershaw

Orange patent-leather "Miss Wonderful" sling-backs, 1960s .... **$35-$55**

Courtesy Timeless Treasures Vintage Clothing Boutique

Delman, wine-colored patent-leather pumps, circa 1995 .... **$200**

Courtesy Rebecca L'Ecuyer

Stuart Weitzman, black platform patent-leather pumps, circa 2007 ....**$200**

Courtesy Rebecca L'Ecuyer

Cole Haan, black patent-leather pumps with velvet bow. Nike Air Soles, circa 2008 .... $200

Courtesy Rebecca L'Ecuyer

Casadei, Italian black leather pumps with orange and white racing stripe, circa 2000 .... **$150**

Courtesy Rebecca L'Ecuyer

Black patent leather pumps with striped bow detail,
circa 1960s... ....**$100**

Courtesy Rebecca L'Ecuyer

Red cobra skin pumps, circa 1940s **$150**

Courtesy Rebecca L'Ecuyers

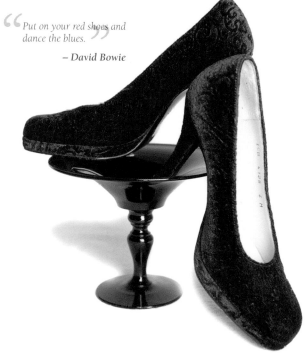

"Put on your red shoes and dance the blues."

– David Bowie

Charles Jourdan, red cut-velvet pumps, circa 1990s **$180**

Courtesy Rebecca L'Ecuyer

High heels were invented by a woman who had been kissed on the forehead.

— Christopher Morley

Pinelli Originals of California, black leather silver-studded pumps with "comma heel," late 1950s – early 1960s **$400**

Caroline Ashleigh Collection

BCBG, gold brocade pumps with jeweled satin bow,
circa 2004 .... **$150**

Courtesy Rebecca L'Ecuyer

Jolene, green suede pumps, circa 1940s.................... .....$100

Courtesy Rebecca L'Ecuyer

L.G. Haig, metallic silver pumps, circa 1960s........................ **$90**

Courtesy Rebecca L'Ecuyer

Connie, red leather pumps, circa 1984 ....**$80**

Courtesy Rebecca L'Ecuyer

I like heels and I do love stilettos, but I don't wear diamonds or makeup when I'm off — I don't walk around dressed in pink diamonds every day.

– Beyonce Knowles

BCBG, gunmetal and black leather stiletto platforms with grosgrain bow detail, circa 2006.. **$300**

Courtesy Rebecca L'Ecuyer

Orange, green, and gold suede pumps with ankle strap, circa 1980s...**$80**

Courtesy Rebecca L'Ecuyer

Town & Country, grey patent-leather pilgrim pumps with silver button detail, circa late 1960s **$150**

Courtesy Rebecca L'Ecuyer

Black patent pilgrim pumps with buckle detail, circa 1960s .. **$400**

Courtesy Rebecca L'Ecuyer

Alden's, green patent-leather stilettos, circa 1960s **$85**

Courtesy Rebecca L'Ecuyer

Chandler Shoe Co., black suede pumps with rhinestone embroidery toe and heel detail, circa 1950s **$100**

Courtesy Rebecca L'Ecuyer

Beverly Feldman, embroidered black silk stiletto pumps with original "Love Connection" box, circa 1950s..................**$175**

Courtesy www.1860-1960.com Julie Guernsey Vintage Fashions

DeLiso Debs, silk pumps with floral decoration, circa 1960s., **$85**

Courtesy Rebecca L'Ecuyer

Deadstock yellow leather "Carina" pumps, 1960s .... **$40-$65**

Courtesy Timeless Treasures Vintage Clothing Boutique

Tooled leather pumps, circa 1980s **$85**

Courtesy Rebecca L'Ecuyer

Brown cobra skin open-toe pumps, circa 1950s................ **$100**

Courtesy Rebecca L'Ecuyer

"Congratulate me! It took all day, but I finally found the perfect pair of alligator pumps to wear to the "Save the Everglades" dinner tonight.

– Hilary Banks, The Fresh Prince of Bel-Air

Jack Schaefer, brown alligator pumps, circa 1940s **$100**

Courtesy Rebecca L'Ecuyer

"Peacock" silver shoes, late 1960s – early 1970s........ **$35-$55**

Courtesy Timeless Treasures Vintage Clothing Boutique

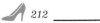

Via Spiga, yellow and red perforated leather pumps
circa 2004 ....**$200**

Courtesy Rebecca L'Ecuyer

Rodger Vivier clear pumps **$140**

Courtesy www.freemansauctions.com, Philadelphia

Roger Vivier, tan leather pumps, 1960s.................... **$125-$200**

Courtesy Timeless Treasures Vintage Clothing Boutique

Black suede and satin ankle collar pumps with velvet bow, circa 1940s.. **$250**

Courtesy Rebecca L'Ecuyer

Carol Ann, black perforated suede patent-leather lace-up booties with scalloped edge detail, circa 1940s **$150**

Courtesy Rebecca LEuayer

Burberry, black patent-leather peek-toe pumps with silver studs,
circa 2008 .... **$400**

Courtesy Rebecca L'Ecuyer

"The boots were amazing. I need to know where they end."

– Paul McCartney, on the full-leg boots shown on Stella McCartney's Paris runway

Black nylon elasticized boot tights, circa 1960s ...., **$500**

Courtesy Rebecca L'Ecuyer

Black suede pumps, circa 1950s **$85**

Courtesy Rebecca L'Ecuyer

Lamb, purple snakeskin and black patent leather stiletto platforms, circa 2008..**$200**

Courtesy Rebecca L'Ecuyer

I think I'll buy these pink shoes — they'll draw attention away from my face.

– Hermione Gingold

Christian Dior, woven hot pink leather platforms, circa 2008 ..**$900**

Courtesy Rebecca L'Ecuyer

Gucci, taupe, gold snakeskin and black suede stiletto platforms, 7", circa 2009 ....,.... .,.... ..**$1,500**

Courtesy Rebecca L'Ecuyer

Miu Miu, black, mint, and red patent leather platforms, circa 2008 ....**$650**

Courtesy Rebecca L'Ecuyer

Chanel, black and white patent-leather ankle strap platforms with stacked heel, circa 2008 .... **$800**

Courtesy Rebecca L'Ecuyer

Silver sequined open-toe stiletto pumps with beaded bow detail, circa 2006 .... **$500**

Courtesy Rebecca L'Ecuyer

Nine West, black leather pumps with ankle cuff detail, circa 2004 ....,.............. **$150**

Courtesy Rebecca L'Ecuyer

Guess, red and white perforated leather strapped pumps, circa 2007 ....**$150**

Courtesy Rebecca L'Ecuyer

Leopoldo Giordano, red, white and black patent-leather sling-back pumps, circa 2004 .... **$200**

Courtesy Rebecca L'Ecuyer

TOBY 5
UPPER LEATHER
MADE IN CHINA

NYLA, multicolored stiletto pumps, circa 2004 .... **$250**

Courtesy Rebecca L'Ecuyer

Aquamarine sparkle shoes with Lucite heel, circa 1970 .... **$400**

Courtesy Sotheby's

Chinese Laundry, hot pink patent leather stiletto pumps, circa 2006 .... **$150**

Courtesy Rebecca L'Ecuyer

Paramount, red satin "No-Heel" pumps with beaded toe detail, circa 1955 ....**$500**

Courtesy Sotheby's

"...the Red Shoes are never tired. They dance ... out onto the street, they dance ... over the mountains and valleys, through fields and forests, through night and day. Time rushes by, love rushes by, life rushes by but the Red Shoes go on."

– Boris Lermontov

Louis Vuitton, black suede with velvet ribbon and hourglass
stiletto heel, punctuated with pearl detail, circa 2009 ...**$1,100**

Courtesy Rebecca L'Ecuyer

Stuart Weitzman, black and gray suede platform pump with bow detail, circa 2009. ....**$400**

Courtesy Rebecca L'Ecuyer

Chanel, black suede and patent leather with pearl detail platform pump, circa 2009...**$900**

Courtesy Rebecca L'Ecuyer

La Rose, raw silk and green leather stiletto pumps with bow detail, circa 1955... **$500 *shoes only***

Courtesy Sotheby's

La Rose, yellow and black plaid pumps with yellow bow detail, circa 1955 .... **$500** *shoes only*

Courtesy Sotheby's

La Rose ad sketch with matching gold and black leather stiletto pumps, circa 1970s .... **$2,500** *sketch and shoes only*

Courtesy Sotheby's

La Rose ad sketch together with matching silk floral-patterned pumps, circa 1955......... ....**$2,500 all**

Courtesy Sotheby's

Herbert Levine classic pumps, purple suede with butterfly buckle, late 1950s – early 1960s .... **$125-$250**

Courtesy Timeless Treasures Vintage Clothing Boutique

La Rose, green suede stiletto pumps, with La Rose ad sketch and Herbert Levine frog ....**$3,000** *all*

Courtesy Sotheby's

Pappagallo, rose-colored turtle skin shoes, circa 1960.. **$350** *shoes only*

Courtesy Sotheby's

Pappagallo, collection of 16 pairs of shoes with floral detail in 10 colors, circa 1970 .... **$125** *each pair*

Courtesy Sotheby's

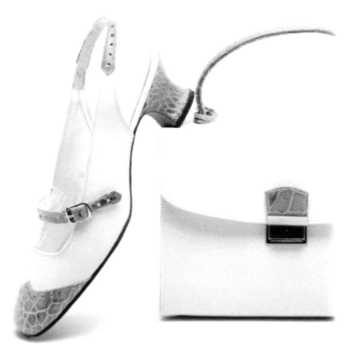

Pappagallo, green turtle skin and white leather sling-back shoes, circa 1960 .... **$350** *shoes only*

Courtesy Sotheby's

Collection of 10 pairs of platform shoes, circa 1970 ... **$350** *each pair*

Courtesy Sotheby's

Martinique Custom Made, hand-painted linen ankle-strap shoes, circa 1940s **$350**

Courtesy www.1860-1960.com Julie Guernsey Vintage Fashions

Schiaparelli, watercolor silk sling-back heels, 1960s **$140**

Courtesy Stacy LoAlbo

Joseph La Rose, multicolored suede pumps, circa 1950s... **$150**

Courtesy Carl and Sharon Ellis

Late '60s maroon suede pumps with black patent leather trim .. **$68**

Courtesy Stacy LoAlbo

Metallic brocade pump in red and gold, late 1940s........... **$185**

From the collection of Vintage with a Twist
Courtesy Stacy LoAlbo

Classic alligator leather platform shoes, 1940s **$225**

Courtesy Stacy LoAlbo

Mr. Seymour, designer points with Lucite bow decoration on
the vamp **$95**

From the collection of Sue Stani at Somerville Center Antiques
Courtesy Stacy LoAlbo

Schiaparelli, aqua satin shoes with embedded rhinestones, late 1950s... **$150**

Courtesy Stacy LoAlbo

Yves Saint Laurent, exotic cobra skin pumps, 1980s, made in Italy.. **$170**

From the collection of What Once Was
Courtesy Stacy LoAlbo

Deep maroon reptile embossed leather pumps, circa 1950s .. **$75**

Courtesy Stacy LoAlbo

Manolo Blahnik, pumps are lizard and snakeskin with a deep
V-cut vamp, 1981...**$800**

From the collection of Vintage with a Twist
Courtesy Stacy LoAlbo

I loved shoes. I loved shoe stores. My devotion to shoes — and that's an understatement — has only grown throughout the years. And I can say without equivocation that's primarily true because of Mr. Manolo Blahnik.

– Sarah Jessica Parker

Manolo Blahnik, signed the inside of these suede pumps with purple feather inserts, circa 1979 .... **$1,500**

From the collection of Vintage with a Twist
Courtesy Stacy LoAlbo

Wild Pair, multicolored snakeskin heels, 1980s **$85**

Courtesy Stacy LoAlbo

Tri-colored metallic leather, suede heels, 1980s **$85**

Courtesy Stacy LoAlbo

Points with multiple layers of brown leather, late 1950s – early 1960s **$75**

Courtesy Stacy LoAlbo

Green lizard skin biscuit-toe pumps, 1940s **$195**

From the collection of Incogneeto
Courtesy Stacy LoAlbo

Brown leather biscuit-toe pumps with gold buckle ornamentation, 1940s **$95**

Courtesy Stacy LoAlbo

Bally leather pumps with gold discs on suede ribbon, 1980s... **$65**

Courtesy Stacy LoAlbo

Joseph, Mod designer shoes with leopard-printed pony hair and classic gold chain vamp, 1970s **$150**

Courtesy Stacy LoAlbo

Selby 5th Avenue, leather penny loafers in an alligator print, 1960s **$68**

Courtesy Stacy LoAlbo

Christian Dior, pumps, 1960s .... **$100** *each pair*

Courtesy www.freemansauctions.com, Philadelphia

Black pump with rhinestone and bead detail, circa 1955 ..... **$95**

Courtesy Stacy LoAlbo

Seymour Troy, leather pumps with lizard skin and open vamp
bow design, 1960s **$95**

Courtesy Stacy LoAlbo

Charles Jourdan, classic duo-tone leather spectators with chunky heels, 1960s **$155**

From the collection of Incogneeto
Courtesy Stacy LoAlbo

Patent leather mod-style platform heels, circa 1970 .... **$75**

Courtesy Stacy LoAlbo

Rodger Vivier pumps..$100 *each pair*

Courtesy www.freemansauctions.com, Philadelphia

Sensible brown suede heels with gold tassels, 1970s **$40**

Courtesy Stacy LoAlbo

Givenchy, pink silk T-strap heels **$135**

From the collection of Incogneeto
Courtesy Stacy LoAlbo

Mario Valentino, multicolored suede spiral-design pumps, circa 1980s.. **$125**

Courtesy Stacy LoAlbo

Herbert Levine, violet suede sling-backs, circa 1960 .... **$235**

From the collection of Vintage with a Twist
Courtesy Stacy LoAlbo

Pupi woven Italian gold leather slippers, 1920s look but circa
1980s **$85**

From the collection of Incogneeto
Courtesy Stacy LoAlbo

Andrew Geller black silk pumps with metallic fish design, circa 1960s **$255**

From the collection of Vintage with a Twist
Courtesy Stacy LoAlbo

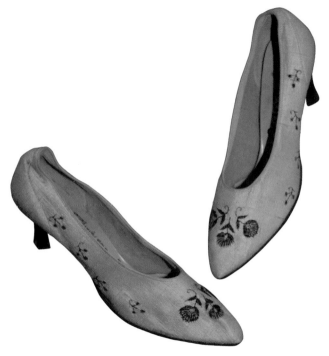

Saks Fifth Avenue, hand-embroidered silk shantung kitten heels, circa 1960 .... **$90**

Courtesy Stacy LoAlbo

Andrea Pfister, designer retro-style lizard skin heels, 1980s   **$75**

Courtesy Stacy LoAlbo

Raphael, lady's green silk evening pumps **$300**

Courtesy www.freemansauctions.com, Philadelphia

Glitter glam shines through on these lavender and blue velvet platforms, 1970s **$160**

Courtesy Stacy LoAlbo

Men's Hornback Crocodile shoes, maker unknown,
1950s ...... ,................................ ... ...**$175-$200**

Courtesy Timeless Treasures Vintage Clothing Boutique

White canvas sling-backs with rainbow-striped wedges,
1970s **$110**

Courtesy Stacy LoAlbo

Leisure Debs, red, white and blue gingham platform wedges, circa 1940s...**$100**

Courtesy www.1860-1960.com Julie Guernsey Vintage Fashions

Blue platform shoes with yellow stitching detail, circa 1970s..**$255**

From the collection of Incogneeto
Courtesy Stacy LoAlbo

Suede platform peep-toe shoes with multi-colored metal studs
in a swirled Art Deco pattern, 1940s.............. .. .. .. ,.. **$350**

From the collection of Incogneeto
Courtesy Stacy LoAlbo

Nina, mile-high leather platform shoes in autumn shades, 1970s **$295**

Courtesy Stacy LoAlbo

Black suede platforms with beaded detail, circa 1940s **$200**

Courtesy Rebecca L'Ecuyer

Lavender and blue velvet platform shoes, circa 1970s ... **$285**

From the collection of Incogneeto
Courtesy Stacy LoAlbo

Beige leather platforms, marked "Terri's", early 1970s **$100**

Courtesy Timeless Treasures Vintage Clothing Boutique

Red leather men's platform shoes, maker unknown, early 1970s... **$225**

Courtesy Timeless Treasures Vintage Clothing Boutique

Spectator, "Cover Girl" red and white platforms, early 1970s...**$250**

Courtesy Timeless Treasures Vintage Clothing Boutique

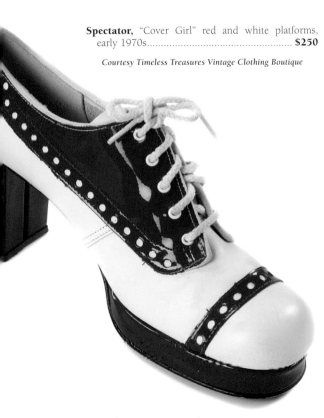

Multicolor leather platforms, made in Greece, early 1970s.....................................**$325**

Courtesy Timeless Treasures Vintage Clothing Boutique

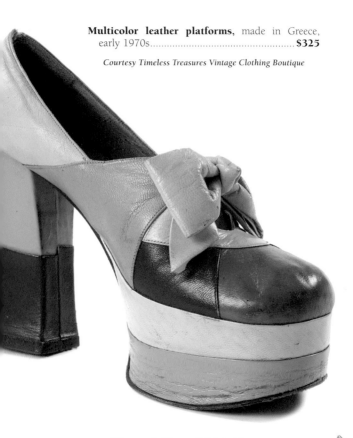

Stuart Weitzman, white leather golf high-top, lace-up boots, circa 1970s..**$150**

Courtesy Rebecca L'Ecuyer

Pro-Shu, patchwork multicolored leather golf shoes, circa 1990s **$250**

Courtesy Rebecca L'Ecuyer

Keds, white leather sneakers with red stitching, circa 1980s..**$200**

Courtesy Rebecca L'Ecuyer

Black canvas high-heel sneakers, circa 1995................. **$100**

Courtesy Rebecca L'Ecuyer

Pink Converse All Star High Tops, circa 2004................. **$90**

Courtesy Rebecca L'Ecuyer

How classy is it for me to wear these pink tennis shoes with my tux?

– Will Ferrell

Boots

Whether they have tapered or spike heels, platform soles, pointed toes, zipper closures or ride high on the thigh, boots take a licking and keep on kicking the fashion world. Singer Nancy Sinatra was largely responsible for popularizing the fad of women wearing boots in the late 1960s. Let's start low and move upward ...

I don't wanna talk about wars between nations. Not right now. Sexy boots/Get on your boots. Yeah, Foxy boots

– U2, "Get On Your Boots"

White leather stiletto boots with orange circular cutout design, circa 2005 .... **$150**

Courtesy Rebecca L'Ecuyer

Guiseppe Zanotti, Italian multi-colored leather boots with dog-tag detail, circa 2000 .... **$400**

Courtesy Rebecca L'Ecuyer

Helen Marlen, black leather mid-calf stiletto boot with cutout detail, circa 2000..**$400**

Courtesy Rebecca L'Ecuyer

B.F. Goodrich, rain boots, circa 1940s.............................. **$100**

Courtesy Rebecca L'Ecuyer

I wish they'd stick with the issues instead of discussing my black go-go boots

— Sarah Palin

High Brows, black and yellow stripe boots, circa 1960s. **$300**

Courtesy Rebecca L'Ecuyer

High Brows, white leather "Go-Go" boots with slant zipper, circa 1960s...**$80**

Courtesy Rebecca L'Ecuyer

Chanel, white leather ankle boot with patent leather trim, circa 2006 ....**$600**

Courtesy Rebecca L'Ecuyer

White leather boots with graphic black trim and peek-toe, circa 1960s **$300**

Courtesy Rebecca L'Ecuyer

Beauty is shoe, shoe beauty.

– Andy Warhol

Mondrian-style "Go-Go" boots, circa 1960s **$400**

Courtesy Rebecca L'Ecuyer

White leather eyelet boots, circa 2000 ... , ... ,.......... **$150**

Courtesy Rebecca L'Ecuyer

Black leather ankle boots with yellow trim, circa 1997 ... **$150**

Courtesy Rebecca L'Ecuyer

Balenciaga, black, white, tan and dove-gray ankle boot, circa 2009 .... **$1,250**

Courtesy Rebecca L'Ecuyer

Baker black patent-leather, lace-up peek-a-boo ankle boot with white piping, circa 2008...**$100**

Courtesy Rebecca L'Ecuyer

Chanel, black patent-leather ankle boots with quilted detail, circa 2007 ....,........ ,,.... **$900**

Courtesy Rebecca L'Ecuyer

Gucci, black velvet ankle boot with gold stud detail, circa 2009 .... **$900**

Courtesy Rebecca L'Ecuyer

Nina Ricci, black suede ankle strap bootie, circa 2008 .... **$850**

Courtesy Rebecca L'Ecuyer

Red and black leather studded child's cowboy boots,
circa 1950s..**$100**

Courtesy www.1860-1960.com Julie Guernsey Vintage Fashions

Blue ostrich skin leather Beatle boots, 1980s **$225**

Courtesy Stacy LoAlbo

Snakeskin boots, made in Italy, circa 1975........................ **$275**

Courtesy Stacy LoAlbo

Italian leather boots, red leather piping and stacked leather heel, circa late 1970s...$95

Courtesy Stacy LoAlbo

Men's alligator boots, 1960s $350

From the collection of What Once Was
Courtesy Stacy LoAlbo

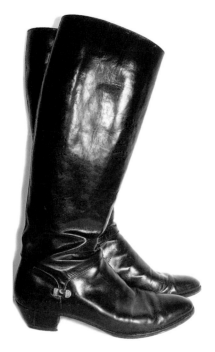

Ferragamo, black leather riding boots, circa late 1980s **$100**

Courtesy www.1860-1960.com Julie Guernsey Vintage Fashions

Gianmarco Brenzi, Italian checkerboard "checks and balances" black and white boot with red ankle strap and padlock detail, circa 2000 .... **$500**

Courtesy Rebecca L'Ecuyer

Kate Spade, black suede boots with patent-leather toe and heel, and black grosgrain bow detail, circa 2006 .... **$350**

Courtesy Rebecca L'Ecuyer

Black and gold spectator lace-up ankle boot,
circa 2004 .... **$350**

Courtesy Rebecca L'Ecuyer

" I think of shoes as architecture for the feet — both share a similar purpose of protection, organization and style. "

– Shoe Designer Martha Davis

Chanel, black patent leather and cloth trim stiletto ankle boot, circa 2007 ....,,................... **$900**

Courtesy Rebecca L'Ecuyer

Previa, black patent-leather boots with silver heels and silver buckle, circa 1980s **$90**

Courtesy Rebecca L'Ecuyer

Vinyl leather boots with nylon zipper, circa 1970s **$75**

Courtesy Rebecca L'Ecuyer

Yves Saint Laurent, brown suede and mink ankle boots, circa 1995 .... **$350**

Courtesy Rebecca L'Ecuyer

Allure, black suede and rabbit-fur-trimmed ankle boot, circa 1995 .... **$200**

Courtesy Rebecca L'Ecuyer

Marc Jacobs, red patent leather ankle boots with black leather strap detail, circa 2005 ....**$500**

Courtesy Rebecca L'Ecuyer

Helen Marlen, black leather ankle boots with black and silver
stiletto airbrushed heel, circa 2000..... ....**$350**

Courtesy Rebecca L'Ecuyer

Nicole Miller, black suede with faux fur lace-up boots, circa 2006 ....**$400**

Courtesy Rebecca L'Ecuyer

Giuliano Venanzi, gold leather and rhinestone buckle boot with stacked heel, circa 1995 ....**$300**

Courtesy Rebecca L'Ecuyer

"Shoes like these should not be locked in a closet! They should be living a life of scandal, and passion!"

– Maggie Feller, "In Her Shoes"

Miu Miu, mustard yellow patent
leather with stacked heel boot,
circa 2003 ....**$300**

Courtesy Rebecca L'Ecuyer

Via Spiga, black patent-leather boot with white heel and sole, circa 2000 .... , ...**$250**

Courtesy Rebecca L'Ecuyer

Roger Vivier, two views of black leather cutout gladiator stiletto boots, circa 2009..**$1,700**

Courtesy Rebecca L'Ecuyer

Cassidy, pony hair and snakeskin animal print boot with pedestal heel, circa 1995..**$3,000**

Courtesy Rebecca L'Ecuyer

Via Spiga, brown pressed-leather boots with stacked heel, circa 2000 .... **$300**

Courtesy Rebecca L'Ecuyer

Daniel Plyner, black leather and rabbit-fur-trimmed cowboy boot
with red flame-stitched snakeskin, circa 2000........ ....**$500**

Courtesy Rebecca L'Ecuyer

Empyre, red vinyl stiletto boots, circa 2000 .... **$150**

Courtesy Rebecca L'Ecuyer

Juicy Couture, silver leather boots, circa 2007 .... **$300**

Courtesy Rebecca L'Ecuyer

Stuart Weitzmen, iridescent orange patent-leather boots, circa 2000 ....**$300**

Courtesy Rebecca L'Ecuyer

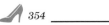

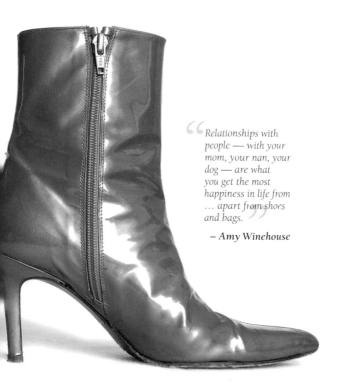

Relationships with people — with your mom, your nan, your dog — are what you get the most happiness in life from … apart from shoes and bags.

– Amy Winehouse

BCBG, leather black and white zebra boots with outside zipper, circa 2000 .... **$300**

Courtesy Rebecca L'Ecuyer

Custom-made white leather boot with gold ankle spur, circa 1985 ....**$500**

Courtesy Rebecca L'Ecuyer

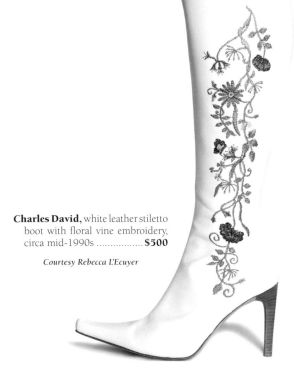

Charles David, white leather stiletto
boot with floral vine embroidery,
circa mid-1990s **$500**

Courtesy Rebecca L'Ecuyer

Steve Madden, white leather mid-calf stiletto boot, circa mid-1990s.....................**$200**

Courtesy Rebecca L'Ecuyer

Gortex Cuissarde, black stiletto boot, circa 2000 ....**$300**

Courtesy Rebecca L'Ecuyer

Marc Jacobs, black leather boots, circa 2005............................ **$350**

Courtesy Rebecca L'Ecuyer

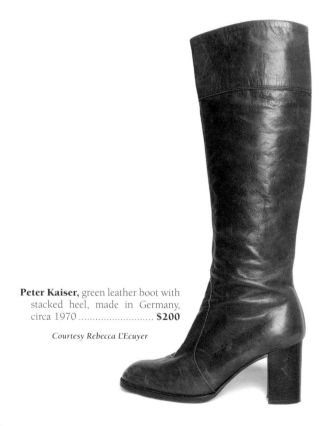

Peter Kaiser, green leather boot with stacked heel, made in Germany, circa 1970 .... **$200**

Courtesy Rebecca L'Ecuyer

Joyce of California, burgundy
leather boot with stacked heel,
circa 1980s **$200**

Courtesy Rebecca L'Ecuyer

Beige suede and leather boot, circa 1970s **$200**

Courtesy Rebecca L'Ecuyer

Cassidy, fuchsia suede stiletto boots with rhinestone detail, circa 2000 .... **$300**

Courtesy Rebecca L'Ecuyer

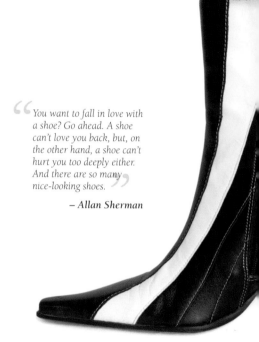

> "You want to fall in love with a shoe? Go ahead. A shoe can't love you back, but, on the other hand, a shoe can't hurt you too deeply either. And there are so many nice-looking shoes."
>
> **– Allan Sherman**

Bronx, black and white striped leather ankle boot, circa 2005 .. **$100**

Courtesy Rebecca L'Ecuyer

Braude, black suede and leather mid-calf boots, circa 2000 .. **$300**

Courtesy Rebecca L'Ecuyer

Burgundy leather boot with gold detail, circa late 1970s..**$350**

Courtesy Rebecca L'Ecuyer

How tall am I? Honey, with hair, heels and attitude I'm through this damned roof.

— RuPaul

Suede cheetah print ankle boots, circa late 1990s **$200**

Courtesy – Rebessa L'Ecuyer

Marc Jacobs, red patent leather and suede ankle boots with ocelot print lining and silver zipper, circa 2005 .... **$500**

Courtesy Rebecca L'Ecuyer

Gianni Versace, ankle boots with cap toe, covered heel, Medusa medallions. Labeled: Gianni Versace..................................**$100**

Courtesy Leslie Hindman Auctioneers

Gianni Versace, black leather military-style boots, 1990s, with Medusa at front. Stamped: Gianni Versace........................**$231**

Courtesy Leslie Hindman Auctioneers

Lanvin, tan kid leather and black patent leather ankle strap boot with silver pedestal heel, circa 2006.............................**$3,000**

Courtesy Rebecca L'Ecuyer

Gianni Versace, red stiletto boots with a zipper at center front
from knee to toe surrounded by a line of rhinestones. Labeled:
Gianni Versace. Made in Italy **$200**

Courtesy Leslie Hindman Auctioneers

Diba, orange patent leather stiletto
boot, circa 2005 ....**$150**

Courtesy Rebecca L'Ecuyer

Diba, hot pink patent leather stiletto boot, circa 2005...**$150**

Courtesy Rebecca L'Ecuyer

Louis Vuitton, black suede and patent leather boots with lace-up velvet bow and hour glass stiletto heel, punctuated with pearl detail, circa 2009..**$2,400**

Courtesy Rebecca L'Ecuyer

Santini Dominici, Italian red plastic cowboy boots, circa 1970s........ .... **$100**

Courtesy Rebecca L'Ecuyer

Pink and blue bejeweled cowboy boots with white leather inset, circa 1990s... **$224**

Courtesy Rebecca L'Ecuyer

There's a snake in my boot!

— Woody, _Toy Story_

Scott Weil's boots, president of Rockmount Ranch Wear Manufacturing Co. Then and now: White leather with gold inlay children's cowboy boots by Goding Boot Co., together with two-tone red and black leather cowboy boots with red flame-stitched inlay by Justin Boot Co. **$400**

Courtesy Rockmount Ranch Wear Manufacturing Co.

The Way We Wore…

The earliest known shoes date from about 8000 to 7000 BC. However, shoes were probably in use long before this, perhaps 30,000 years ago.

Ancient designs were simple "foot bags" of leather to protect the feet from rocks, debris and cold. By the Middle Ages, "turn-shoes" had been developed with toggled flaps or drawstrings to tighten the leather around the foot for a better fit. In Japan, wooden shoes mounted on thin blocks three or four inches high have been worn for centuries.

As Europe gained in wealth and power, fancy shoes became status symbols. Eventually the modern shoe, with a sewn-on sole, was devised. Since the 17th century, most leather shoes have used a sewn-on sole.

"Waldron/Maker/Basinghall Street/ London", ivory cannelle silk woven with green vinery slippers with clogs labeled, circa 1790 .... **$11,750**

Courtesy Doyle New York, Appraisers & Auctioneers

Until around 1800, shoes were made without differentiation for the left or right foot. Such shoes were called "straights." Nineteenth century button or lace-up boots were tight fitting and calf defining, which imitated the laced corsets that nipped in the waist and shaped the torso.

We also associate shoes with good luck and prosperity and, as such, they play a role in many marriage ceremonies in various cultures around the globe. Vestiges of this custom still exist in our own modern culture as seen in the habit of tying shoes to the bumper of the newlywed's car.

Shoe size has a long been associated with attractiveness and sex appeal. Over the ages, women have sometimes gone to painful lengths to make their feet appear to be smaller. The most extreme example of this can be seen in the practice of foot-binding, which was popular in China up until the first half of the 20th century. Some social anthropologists suggest that this custom is the actual origin of the "Cinderella" story.

Silk embroidered Lotus shoes for bound feet, circa 1900...**$100**

Courtesy www.1860-1960.com Julie Guernsey Vintage Fashions

Black leather Lotus shoes for bound feet, circa 1900....... **$100**

Caroline Ashleigh Collection

Civil War brogans, black leather, square-toed pair, stamped "W.H. King/Insp. Cin." **$23,900**

Courtesy Heritage Auction Galleries

Pair of un-issued "Bootees." Sometimes called brogans, these shoes were part of soldiering in the Civil War. This pair appears to be un-issued, with a smooth exterior of blackened leather that rises high upon the ankle, and a thin leather lining. Each shoe has three eyelets reinforced with thin metal grommets, with the original brown cord ties remaining in place. The wooden-pegged soles and metal-pegged heels are virtually unworn. Difficult to find such footwear in this condition..**$6,572**

Courtesy Heritage Auction Galleries

Ottoman Turk gold metallic thread slipper shoes, circa 1900 .. **$100**

Courtesy www.1860-1960.com Julie Guernsey Vintage Fashions

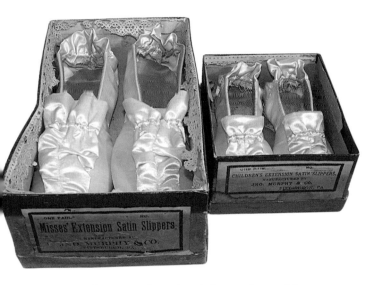

Victorian white satin slipper burial shoes and original boxes,
circa 1860s...**$300** *each pair*

Courtesy www.1860-1960.com Julie Guernsey Vintage Fashions

Edwardian brown suede "T.A. Chapman" shoes .... **$85-$150**

Courtesy Timeless Treasures Vintage Clothing Boutique

Six pairs of German character doll shoes, late 19th century,
leather ....**$373** *all*

James D. Julia Auctioneers, Fairfield, Me.; www.jamesdjulia.com

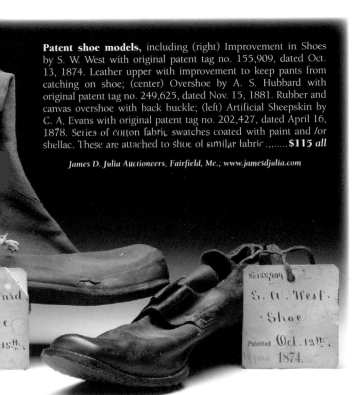

Patent shoe models, including (right) Improvement in Shoes by S. W. West with original patent tag no. 155,909, dated Oct. 13, 1874. Leather upper with improvement to keep pants from catching on shoe; (center) Overshoe by A. S. Hubbard with original patent tag no. 249,625, dated Nov. 15, 1881. Rubber and canvas overshoe with back buckle; (left) Artificial Sheepskin by C. A. Evans with original patent tag no. 202,427, dated April 16, 1878. Series of cotton fabric swatches coated with paint and /or shellac. These are attached to shoe of similar fabric .,.....**$115 all**

James D. Julia Auctioneers, Fairfield, Me.; www.jamesdjulia.com

Victorian black button shoes with cutout latticework straps and cut steel beaded detail, circa 1900............................. **$450**

Courtesy www.1860-1960.com Julie Guernsey Vintage Fashions

Victorian black leather cross-strapped, high-button boots with
cut-steel beaded appliqué detail on vamp, circa 1900.........**$600**

Courtesy www.1860-1960.com Julie Guernsey Vintage Fashions

Edwardian midnight-blue velvet high-top button boots with white piping, circa 1905..**$150**

Courtesy www.1860-1960.com Julie Guernsey Vintage Fashions

Victorian black silk high button boots, circa 1900 .... **$400**

Courtesy www.1860-1960.com Julie Guernsey Vintage Fashions

Victorian two-tone brown leather and wool lace-up boots with
punch-work toe detail, circa 1900.................................**$200**

Courtesy www.1860-1960.com Julie Guernsey Vintage Fashions

Victorian white canvas high top lace-up boots, circa 1900 .. **$150**

Courtesy www.1860-1960.com Julie Guernsey Vintage Fashions

Victorian brown leather and silk brocade paisley fabric boots
with fleur-de-lis leather trim, circa 1870 .... **$250**

Courtesy www.1860-1960.com Julie Guernsey Vintage Fashions

Sautters & Son, Victorian gray wool and leather lade-up boots
with punch-work toe detail, New York, circa 1900 .... **$200**

Courtesy www.1860-1960.com Julie Guernsey Vintage Fashions

Victorian black velvet rabbit-fur-lined carriage boots, circa 1880 ....**$150**

Courtesy www.1860-1960.com Julie Guernsey Vintage Fashions

Victorian black leather high-button child's fashion boots with scalloped edge, circa 1870s..**$200**

Courtesy www.1860-1960.com Julie Guernsey Vintage Fashions

Vintage satin silk slippers with hand-embroidered rabbits... **$90**

Courtesy Stacy LoAlbo

Victorian suede cross-strapped button shoes with cut-steel beaded appliqués on vamp..**$200**

Courtesy Carl and Sharon Ellis

Victorian tan and black high-button baby shoes, circa 1900 .. **$200**

Courtesy www.1860-1960.com Julie Guernsey Vintage Fashions

Victorian child's red leather button boots with white porcelain
buttons and silk tassel trim, circa 1900 .... **$200**

Courtesy www.1860-1960.com Julie Guernsey Vintage Fashions

Red silk child's Chinese tiger shoes, circa 1940s............. **$100**

Courtesy www.1860-1960.com Julie Guernsey Vintage

Tibetan multicolored boot with leather sole, circa 1900s....**$125**

Caroline Ashleigh Collection

Baby booties with fur trim and original box by Baby Deer, circa 1950s. Original price $3.95 .... **$100**

Courtesy Rebecca L'Ecuyer

Cozyfoot, baby booties with original box, circa 1930s.......... **$80**

Courtesy Rebecca L'Ecuyer

Edwardian lady's red cotton canvas lace-up bathing boots, circa 1915 .... **$250**

Courtesy www.1860-1960.com Julie Guernsey Vintage Fashions

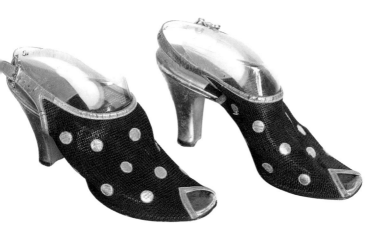

Black mesh sling-back evening sandals with applied gold polka
dots, rhinestone buckle and cutout toe, circa 1920s **$500**

Courtesy Rebecca L'Ecuyer

Sax of Detroit, gold leather T-strap evening sandals with amber rhinestone buckle and Louis heel, circa 1920s **$500**

Courtesy Rebecca L'Ecuyer

Gold and silver hand-stitched leather T-strap evening sandals
with open toe and rhinestone buckle, circa 1920s **$500**

Courtesy Rebecca L'Ecuyer

Delman, mint green and magenta silk evening sandals with gold leather trim, circa 1920s..**$500**

Courtesy Rebecca L'Ecuyer

T-strap leather heels with cut out details, 1920s...............**$175**

Courtesy Stacy LoAlbo

Black silk and metallic lamé evening shoes, circa 1920s .. **$200**

Courtesy www.1860-1960.com Julie Guernsey Vintage Fashions

La Parisienne, blue and silver brocade-style evening slipper with button strap closure and Louis heel, circa 1920 .... **$250**

Courtesy www.1860-1960.com Julie Guernsey Vintage Fashions

Chocolate brown pumps, with leather strip detailing across the vamp and silk grosgrain ribbon ties, late 1920s **$155**

From the collection of Incogneeto
Courtesy Stacy LoAlbo

Dance shoes with a swirled bit of snakeskin and a "Louis"-shaped heel, early 1920s **$175**

Courtesy Stacy LoAlbo

Blue leather 1930s heels with intricate detail across the vamp
and bows..**$150**

From the collection of Kitsch 'n' Wear
Courtesy Stacy LoAlbo

Blue silk embroidered sling-back pumps, 1930s................... **$150**

Courtesy www.1860-1960.com Julie Guernsey Vintage Fashions

Famous Footwear

ONCE UPON A TIME ...

Shoes have a mythical, magical quality which is why it is no accident that they are a common theme in some of our most enduring children's stories and fairy tales such as "Cinderella," "The Wizard of Oz," "The Shoemaker and the Elves" and "Puss in Boots."

Though the Cinderella theme may have originated in classical antiquity, the most famous version was written by Charles Perrault in 1697. The popularity of his tale was due to his additions to the story, including the pumpkin, the fairy-godmother and the introduction of glass slippers.

In L. Frank Baum's first "Oz" book, published in 1900, the Good Witch of the North comes with the Munchkins to greet Dorothy and she gives Dorothy the pair of silver (not ruby) shoes that the Wicked Witch of the East had been wearing when she was killed.

Elvis Presley's black patent-leather stage boots, Italian-made with zipper closures, owned and worn onstage by Elvis. Accompanied by a letter of provenance from Elvis' cousin, Jerry Presley **$7,170**

Courtesy Heritage Auction Galleries

Judy Garland wearing the ruby slippers and Ray Bolger
in a publicity still from "The Wizard of Oz."

Courtesy Heritage Auction Galleries

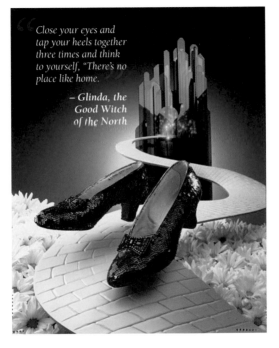

Close your eyes and tap your heels together three times and think to yourself, "There's no place like home.

– Glinda, the Good Witch of the North

Ruby Slippers from "The Wizard of Oz," made by Gilbert Adrian, 1939 ... .**$666,000**

Library of Congress

Red leather vintage clown shoes, circa 1950s.................. **$500**

Caroline Ashleigh Collection

*These shoes once belonged to Milky the Clown, played by
Clarence Cummings Jr. (1912-1994). Milky was a staple
in Detroit children's television in the 1950s and '60s.*

Ronald Reagan "Knute Rockne" football cleats. Worn by Reagan in his role of George "The Gipper" Gipp in the 1940 biopic, "Knute Rockne All American."............................**$10,157**

Courtesy Heritage Auction Galleries

 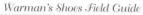

James Cagney's spats worn in the 1942 film, "Yankee Doodle Dandy."... **$4,000**

Courtesy Doyle New York, Appraisers & Auctioneers

1962 Mantle & Maris sneakers in original box. In the wake of perhaps the most exciting season in Yankee history, the M&M boys became the darlings of Madison Avenue as well as the Bronx. One savvy marketer secured the rights to the pair's names and images to endorse sneakers. These size 11 shoes bear the Mantle/Maris logo. The box, with its 1962 copyright clearly marked, features facsimile autographs...**$1,015**

Courtesy Heritage Auction Galleries

It's an unlisted shoe, Operator!

– Maxwell Smart, "Get Smart"

"Get Smart" signed shoe phone and cap. An official Nick At Nite shoe phone signed by Don Adams in silver marker, along with a cap signed by Adams, Dick Gautier and Bernie Kopell in black marker ....**$180** *all*

Courtesy Heritage Auction Galleries

Phyllis Diller signed print of her painting titled, "Martha's Shoe," no. 8 in a limited edition of 500, presented by the comedienne as a gift to Kaye Ballard. Also included is the handwritten note in black ballpoint from Diller to Ballard that accompanied the piece .. **$155**

Courtesy Heritage Auction Galleries

Chubby Checker's checked boots, and an autographed photo, in a shabowbox frame.........................**$1,375**

Courtesy www.juliensauctions.com

Mamie Dowd Eisenhower: Pink hat, gloves and shoes with a photograph of Ike in a traveling frame. The hat, in Mrs. Eisenhower's trademark pink and covered in ostrich feathers, was made by Laddie Northridge, New York. The cloth gloves are 10" long and unmarked. The shoes, 6½ B X959 / AA heel and marked on the liner, "Made Expressly for Mrs. Dwight D. Eisenhower", are in an A.S. Beck Cameo Room box. The red leather traveling frame has a heart-shaped opening with a photograph of a smiling President Eisenhower .... **$1,075** *all*

Courtesy Heritage Auction Galleries

Harry S. Truman souvenir painted wooden shoes, 3 1/2" x 9". The right shoe is painted with the flag of the United States and the Netherlands with a riband below bearing the words, "President Truman + Koningin Juliana Souvenir 1949". Behind the flags are painted a Dutch windmill and an artist's rendering of the United Nations headquarters building. The left shoe is painted with the flags of the United States and Belgium with a riband below bearing the words, "Prins Regent Karel + President Truman Souvenir 1949". Behind the flags are painted a Belgian roadside shrine and an artist's rendering of the United Nations headquarters building **$180**

Courtesy Heritage Auction Galleries

"Rocky IV" Sylvester Stallone costume boxing shoes.
A pair of white Adidas boxing shoes worn by Stallone in the
1985 sequel, with an MGM costume tag sewn into the tongue of
the right shoe...... .... **$1,900**

Courtesy Heritage Auction Galleries

One should either be a work of art, or wear a work of art.

– Oscar Wilde

Eleanor Powell dancing shoes. Former wife of Glenn Ford, Eleanor Powell made the transition from the Broadway stage to Hollywood soundstage in 1935, where her tap dancing skills quickly made her a star. Powell went on to star opposite many of the decade's top leading men such as Jimmy Stewart, George Murphy, Nelson Eddy, Robert Young and Fred Astaire. This pair of fuchsia tap shoes was owned and worn by Powell opposite Astaire in the musical "Broadway Melody of 1940." Encased in a display box with a small plaque reading, "Eleanor Powell/Broadway Melody 1940/MGM." The shoes show some wear and cracking from age and rigorous use, and are affixed to the case's wooden base by a screw through each heel. From the Glenn Ford Estate...................**$2,000**

Courtesy Heritage Auction Galleries

Glenn Ford's horseshoes from Henry Fonda.
A pair of chrome horseshoes mounted on a plaque
with a metal plate reading, "To Glenn from Hank
and 'Ol' Fooler'", a gift to Ford from friend and
co-star Henry Fonda. Ol' Fooler was the roan horse
that costarred with Ford and Fonda in the 1964
film, "The Rounders" — Ford's favorite Western.
From the Glenn Ford Estate **$500**

Courtesy Heritage Auction Galleries

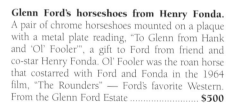

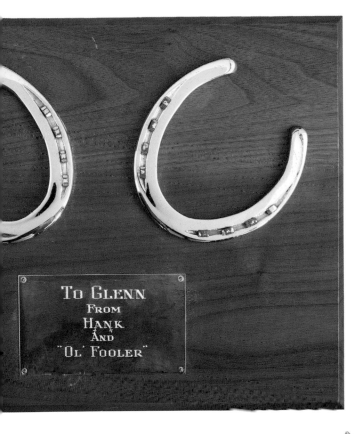

To Glenn
From
Hank
And
"Ol' Fooler"

Ernie Kovacs' cowboy props from cigar commercial. Includes a pair of brown cowboy boots, black cowboy hat and prop six-shooter, used by Kovacs' counterpart in one of his TV commercial for Dutch Masters brand cigars ....**$420** *all*

Courtesy Heritage Auction Galleries

Dwight Yoakum signed cowboy boots, plus
signed photograph **$2,000**

Courtesy www.juliensauctions.com

Barbra Streisand white cowboy boots by Francois Villon of Italy...... ....,...... ....**$300**

Courtesy www.juliensauctions.com

Buddy Ebsen's tap shoes. As a child, Buddy Ebsen and his sisters learned to dance at a studio run by his father in Orlando, Fla. He began dancing in vaudeville dancer and was able to parlay that into roles on Broadway and eventually musical films of the 1930s. He used this pair of tap shoes during later portions of his career, in film and during public appearances. The brown and white leather shoes feature steel taps in the heels, wooden toe taps and flap closures. From the Buddy Ebsen Estate **$475**

Courtesy Heritage Auction Galleries

Jerry Lee Lewis certainly used his feet more than most any other Rockabilly cat, even playing some notes on the piano with the heel of his shoe. These 9 1/2 Frank Brothers white-top loafers have seen their fair share of stomping, jumping and standing on the piano. With a letter of provenance from Lewis' former employee, confirming that they belonged to "The Killer." **$1,150**

Courtesy Heritage Auction Galleries

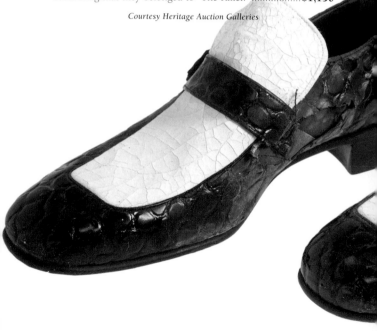

Raquel Welch costume roller skates from "Kansas City Bomber," size 6 1/2, worn by Welch in the 1972 roller drama. An MGM costume label bearing Welch's name is sewn onto the tongue of the left skate... **$775; Poster, $30**

Courtesy Heritage Auction Galleries

Jimi Hendrix stage-worn boots. Accompanied by two large-format photographs (one shown) of Hendrix wearing the boots onstage at Golden Gate Park on June 27, 1967, just days after his legendary performance at the Monterey Pop Festival. The shots were taken by photographer James Marshall, who signed and dated the photographs' mat boards. The B&W images provide two views of Hendrix wearing the boots .... **$21,500** *all*

Courtesy Heritage Auction Galleries

Apollo 13-flown pair of "Booties" from the personal collection of Mission Commander James Lovell. Beta cloth boots with dual snap closures and a 3 1/2" diameter area of Velcro on the bottom. There is a tag sewn in each with the following information: "Boot Assy. R. H. (L. H.)/ BW-1062-002/ Size: 10 S/N: 1110/ Subject: Lovell/ Contract No.: NAS 9-8309/ Date of Mfg.: 3-3-69/ Mfg. By: B. Welson Co." These would have been the footwear for Lovell while on board ship and he has certified the left boot on the toe area: "Apollo 13 in-flight suit booties used in Acquarius S/C". On their storage bag is a label that he has certified and signed: "Interior Apollo 13 booties- Flown James Lovell". Includes a signed letter of authenticity from Lovell stating, "[These] Internal flight suit beta cloth booties - worn during flight of Apollo 13 [were] flown on board the Apollo 13 Command Module Odyssey during its perilous flight around the moon April 11-17, 1970." **$18,000**

Courtesy Heritage Auction Galleries

Cher's faux leopard-trimmed shoes. A pair of black heels with
faux snow leopard trim from Cher's personal wardrobe.... **$125**

Courtesy Heritage Auction Galleries

How strange, when your father's wearing women's clothes and platform shoes, that a pair of loafers looks incredible.

– Moon Unit Zappa

Collection of boots owned by Cher,
clockwise from top:

Leopard print $800

Manolo Blahnik $400

Jim Francofore $500

Denim $425

Christian Dior $1,600

Leather $425

Manolo Blahnik $650

Manolo Blahnik $500

Gianni Versace $600

Guido Pasquali $600

Robert Cavalli $900

Dolce & Gabbana $950

Courtesy www.juliensauctions.com

Barbara Mandrell owned and worn boots, Italian-made turquoise suede and leather...**$180**

Courtesy Heritage Auction Galleries

Early 1970's Bobby Orr game-worn skates. CCM Tackaberry
Prolite skates bearing number "4"..................................**$6,575**

Courtesy Heritage Auction Galleries

1996-97 Michael Jordan sneakers, worn during the Bulls' fifth World Championship season. Custom Nike high-tops; right shoe is autographed by Jordan in black felt tip..... **$3,350**

Courtesy Heritage Auction Galleries

"It's gotta be the shoes."

*– Spike Lee, on what made Michael Jordan
such a great basketball player*

Scottie Pippen game-worn and signed shoes with signed photograph. White Nike Air Flights, each shoe has been signed by Pippen .... **$250** *with photo*

Courtesy Heritage Auction Galleries

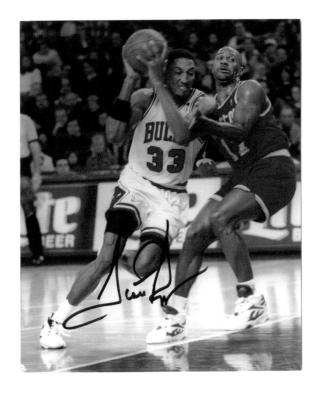

THE
JOHNSTON & MURPHY
SHOE

"THE SHOE WITH A MEMORY"

Remember to retain its pleasure, comfort
and shape after endless wearings becau
it is built with the finest materials an
meticulous workmanship.

Bob Hope red and white patent leather golf shoes with original box...**$900**

Courtesy www.juliensauctions.com

1957 Jim Brown Syracuse University bronzed game-worn cleat. It was dipped in bronze and affixed to a wooden mount by a Long Island, N.Y., civic club, which added an engraved plaque that reads, "Presented to Jimmy Brown, Feb. 6, 1957 By Manhasset Post 304, American Legion.".... **$1,300**

Courtesy Heritage Auction Galleries

U2's The Edge stage-worn blue and white leather tennis shoes, worn in performance in Dublin......................................**$7,000**

Courtesy www.juliensauctions.com

"Gi-normous" size 18 men's leather shoes, worn by a giant in
the circus, circa late 1960s, early 1970s **$200**

Caroline Ashleigh Collection

Everybody's Got Sole

The shoe has been used as art inspiration and metaphor. Our journey wraps up with some examples of shoe-related memorabilia, both funky and fine.

Howard Finster (American 1916-2001), If A Shoe Fits, Wear It, 1995, mixed media on wood. 10 1/2" x 17 1/2", signed on reverse: Howard; numbered 37,342 .... **$350**

Courtesy Heritage Auction Galleries

Tortoise shell art glass boot and purse ensemble .... **$200** *set*

Courtesy Rebecca L'Ecuyer

"When I am an old woman I shall wear purple, with a red hat which doesn't go and doesn't suit me, and I shall spend my pension on brandy and summer gloves, and satin sandals, and say we've no money for butter."

– Jenny Joseph

Macerated lady's shoe, early 1900s. The label reads, "Made of U.S. National Greenbacks redeemed and macerated at U.S. Treasury. Manufactured at 14th St. N.W., Washington, D.C." **$4,000**

Courtesy Heritage Auction Galleries

Adlai Stevenson, "Hole in the Shoe" brass paperweight,
4 1/4" long **$260**

Courtesy Heritage Auction Galleries

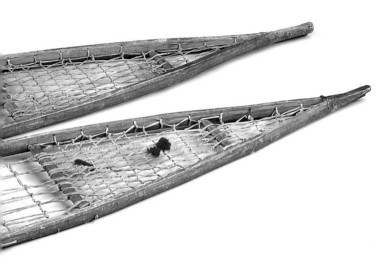

Cree model wood and hide snowshoes, circa 1900, each composed of wood frame, tightly strung with sinew, embellished with tufts of red and green wool, 24 3/4" long each............... **$60**

Courtesy Heritage Auction Galleries

American folk-art shoeshine box, early 20th century, paint-decorated oak, pine and sheet-metal in the form of a shoe. The hinged, sloping lid serving as a footrest opening to the storage interior; painted in silver with black trim, the outline of sole and heel retains studs once fastening a leather sole (now absent), 8" x 17 3/4" x 5". Retains original paint and fittings, with old patina **$345**

James D. Julia Auctioneers, Fairfield, Me.; www.jamesdjulia.com

Silver snuffbox, unknown maker, American, 19th century, in the form of a shoe, with embossed decoration of forest animals. Silver gilt interior, marked "Sterling", 2 3/4" long, 1 troy ounce **$90**

Courtesy Heritage Auction Galleries

Shoehorn, Whiting Manufacturing Co., Providence, R.I., circa 1890, marked, "Whiting, Sterling, 3", 7 1/2" long, 2.83 troy ounces..**$1,015**

Courtesy Heritage Auction Galleries

Western boot cobblers toolbox, primitive handmade box containing tools of the trade for the shoe or boot repairman; 12" x 13" x 8", circa 1890s.. **$90**

Courtesy Heritage Auction Galleries

Red Goose Shoes plaster figurine on green base, 11 1/4" h... **$115**

Courtesy James D. Julia Auctioneers, Fairfield, Maine; www.JuliaAuctions.com

Painting signed "Fox" (American 20th Century), Pink Dress With
New Shoes, oil on canvas, 25 1/2" x 23", signed lower left..**$260**

Courtesy Heritage Auction Galleries

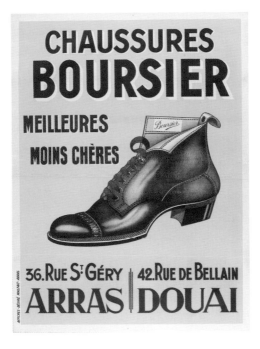

French advertising poster, Boursier, 1920s, 45 1/2" x 59".. **$38**

Courtesy Heritage Auction Galleries

Peter Driben (American, 1902-1968), Silk Stockings and High Heels, Wink cover, September 1948, oil on board, 31" x 21", signed lower right **$16,730**

Courtesy Heritage Auction Galleries

You see, in this country, my husband is a very powerful man. He's a shoe salesman.

– Peg Bundy, "Married With Children"

Jack Davis roller-skating shoe salesman illustration original art (undated). High-rolling illustration by Davis, a Mad magazine regular, with an image area of 8" x 12". Ink with wash on heavy illustration paper, signed by the artist at the lower right **$130**

Courtesy Heritage Auction Galleries

Cabinet card depicting a shoeshine boy and his young client **$920**

Courtesy Heritage Auction Galleries

The Red Shoes (Eagle Lion, 1948). Lobby Card (11" X 14"). Fantasy. Starring Moira Shearer, Marius Goring, Anton Walbrook and Robert Helpmann. Directed by Michael Powell and Emeric Pressburger... **$60**

Courtesy Heritage Auction Galleries

BILL ROBINSON . . . 20th CENTURY-FOX PLAYER

Bill "Bojangles" Robinson photograph (20th Century Fox, 1935), 8" x 10". Vintage black and white, single weight, glossy publicity photo of Bill Robinson holding his dancing shoes. On the back is a note that describes his owning the same pair of dancing shoes for 30 years **$180**

Courtesy Heritage Auction Galleries

Tight Shoes (Universal, 1941). One Sheet (27" X 41"). Starring John Howard, Binnie Barnes, Broderick Crawford, Leo Carrillo, Anne Gwynne, and Shemp Howard...**$16**

Courtesy Heritage Auction Galleries

The Man with One Red Shoe (20th Century Fox, 1985). One Sheet (27" X 41") Style A **$10**

Courtesy Heritage Auction Galleries

Buster Brown Shoes neon sign, one-sided, electrified porcelain, depicts Buster Brown and his faithful companion, Tige. When the sign is turned on, Buster not only lights up but he also winks........**$4,200**

James D. Julia Auctioneers, Fairfield, Me.; www.jamesdjulia.com

Buster Brown Shoes whistle premium, tin lithograph whistle given as an advertising premium by the makers of Buster Brown Shoes. Marked "Made in Germany" **$30**

Courtesy Heritage Auction Galleries

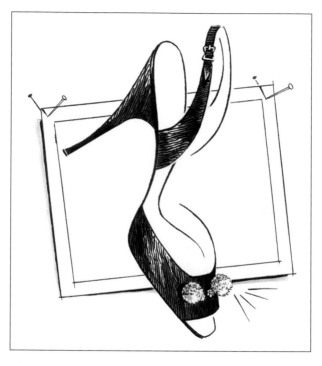

La Rose ad sketch, "Pin-Up Sling back," circa 1955.......**$2,500**

Courtesy Sotheby's

Lady's leg lamp, circa 1995... **$85**

Courtesy Rebecca L'Ecuyer

Resources

INTERNET

www.1860-1960.com

www.vintagefashionguild.com

www.theshoegoddess.com

www.zappos.com

www.whowhatwear.com

www.charlesjourdan.com

www.christianlouboutin.fr

www.gina.com

www.jimmychoo.com

www.manoloblahnik.com

www.rogervivier.com

www.viviennewestwoodonline.co.uk

www.terryhavilland.com

www.stuartweitzman.com

www.katespade.com

www.appraiseyourart.com

www.auctionyourart.com

AUCTION HOUSES

Julien's Auctions, Los Angeles; www.juliensauctions.com

Heritage Auction Galleries, Dallas; www.HA.com

Sotheby's New York; www.sothebys.com

Doyle New York; www.doylenewyork.com

Freeman's Auctioneers, Philadelphia; www.freemansauction.com

Leslie Hindman Auctioneers, Chicago; www.lesliehindman.com

James D. Julia Auctioneers, Fairfield, Me.; www.jamesdjulia.com

MUSEUMS

Bata Shoe Museum, Toronto; www.batashoemuseum.ca

Costume Institute, Metropolitan Museum of Art, New York;
www.metmuseum.org/Works_of_Art/the_costume_institute

Fashion Institute of Technology Museum,
New York; www.fitnyc.edu

Kent State University Museum, Kent,
Ohio; www.kent.edu/museum

Vintage Fashion Museum, Abilene, Kan.; www.abilenekansas.org

THE SOLEFUL EXCHANGE®

"Boy with First Pair of New Shoes" by Gerald Waller. This photo appeared in a 1946 issue of Life magazine. It shows a little boy by the name of Werfel, a 6-year-old war orphan, who had just received a new pair of shoes from the American Red Cross. To continue this tradition, author Caroline Ashleigh has established the "Soleful Exchange®" to provide shoes to the homeless in major urban centers throughout the United States. To find out more about the "Soleful Exchange®", please contact Ashleigh at info@appraiseyourart.com

Photo used by permission of the Maryland Historical Society

About the Author

Recognized among industry peers for her extensive work and deep knowledge within the art and antique industry, Caroline Ashleigh has appeared as an appraiser on the popular television show, Antiques Roadshow, from 1997 to the present, and has been featured in publications such as Forbes Magazine, The New York Times, and Arts and Antiques Magazine. Throughout her professional career, Ashleigh has claimed some of the biggest names in the collecting world as clients, including working relationships with respected auction houses, major museums, and celebrity collections. Ashleigh is also a noted public speaker and lectures extensively on many facets of appraising and collecting.

A certified member of the Appraisers Association of America and graduate of New York University's Appraisal Studies Program in Fine and Decorative Arts, Ashleigh is currently working closely with NYU and the Appraisers Association of America to develop an accredited online course for appraisers.

Index

Alden's, 204

Alfred Ruby Inc., 64

Allure, 341

Andrea Pfister, 180, 285

Andrew Geller, 283

Andy Warhol, 6, 319

B.F. Goodrich, 314

Balenciaga, 323

Bally, 269

BCBG, 96, 122, 128, 196, 200, 356

Bebe, 80, 134

Beverly Feldman, 161, 206

Braude, 368

Bronx, 366, 435

Burberry, 218

Buster Brown, 500-501

Carina, 208

Carol Ann, 217

Casadei, 190

Cassidy, 349, 365

Chandler, 172, 205

Chanel, 61, 117, 183, 225, 239, 317, 325, 337

Charles David, 106-107, 358

Charles Jourdan, 75, 118, 193, 275

Chinese Laundry, 111, 132, 233

Christian Dior, 222, 272, 464

Civil War, 386-387

Claudia Cuiti, 113

Cole Haan, 189

Connie, 83, 199

Converse, 308

Cookies, 105

Cover Girl, 301

Cuissarde, 360

Daniel Plyner, 351

Delman, 187, 418

Di Orsini, 44

Diba, 376-377

Dior, 35, 222, 272, 464

Dolce and Gabbana, 51

Edwardian, 9, 390, 398, 414

Empyre, 352

Enzo Angiolini, 102

Escapezios, 130

Evins, 175
Exclusive, 52
Ferantino, 177
Ferncraft Exclusives, 144
Fluxa, 18
Gainsborough, 55, 59
Garolini, 45
Gianmarco Brenzi, 334
Giuliano Venanzi, 345
Givenchy, 279
Gucci, 81, 88, 182, 223, 326
Guess, 8, 228
Guiseppe Zanotti, 26, 312
Herbert Burr, 174
Herbert Levine, 245-246, 281
High Brows, 315-316
I. Miller, 146
Jack Schaefer, 211
Jan Josef, 34
Jolene, 197
Joyce of California, 363
Juicy Couture, 353
Kate Spade, 38, 335
Keds, 306
Kenneth Cole, 95
Kristoff, 98

L.G. Haig, 198
L'Autre Chose, 78
La Parisienne, 421
La Rose, 240-243, 246, 254, 502
Lamb, 221
Lanvin, 22, 374
Leopoldo Giordano, 229
Louis Vuitton, 25, 29, 236, 378
Lucite, 142-143, 147-148, 181, 232, 258
Manolo Blahnik, 77, 85, 101, 114, 262-263, 464
Marc Jacobs, 41, 60, 79, 127, 169, 194, 342, 361, 371
Martinique, 58, 252
Mary Janes, 11, 169
Michael Kors, 86, 168
Miss Wonderful, 186
Miu Miu, 23-24, 91, 94, 97, 224, 346
Moda Spana, 112
Mosquitos, 76
Mr. Seymour, 258
Nicole Miller, 344
Nike, 189, 469-470
Nina, 55, 294, 327

Nina Ricci, 327

Nine West, 15, 123, 126, 137, 166, 227

NYLA, 231

Oliver, 76

Palizzio, 173

Palter DeLiso, 142

Pappagallo, 247-249

Paputsi, 110

Paramount, 234

Peacock, 212

Peter Kaiser, 302

Petite Custom Made Shoes, 57

Pierre Hardy, 21

Pinelli Originals of California, 195

Prada, 20, 30, 120

Previa, 338

Pro-Shu, 305

Pucci, 31, 74

Red Goose, 489

Renee Caovilla, 184

Rockmount Ranch Wear Manufacturing Co., 381

Roger Vivier, 215, 348

Saks Fifth Avenue, 67, 284

Saks Kay Shoe Salon, 68

Santini Dominici, 379

Sax of Detroit, 416

Schiaparelli, 253, 259

Selby 5th Avenue, 271

Sensual Steps, 124

Sesto Meucci, 109

Seymour Troy, 274

Spring-O-Lator, 12, 32, 36

Steve Madden, 100, 163, 359

Stuart Weitzman, 77, 165, 167, 179, 188, 237, 304

T.A. Chapman, 390

Terri's, 297

Terry de Havilland, 87

Thom McAn, 71

Town & Country, 202

Valenciaga, 27

Valentino, 82, 280

Versace, 372-373, 375, 464

Via Spiga, 19, 121, 135, 213, 347, 350

Victorian, 389, 396-397, 399-405, 407-409

Wild Pair, 264

Young and Fair Casuals, 53

Yves Saint Laurent, 16, 28, 89, 260, 340

More Fabulous Guides to Vintage Flair